BASEBALL
TOP 10

STANDARD BERRA
Yankees catcher Yogi Berra appeared in more World Series games than any other player. Here he applies the tag in a play from the 1950 World Series.

MAJOR LEAGUE BASEBALL™

BASEBALL TOP 10

Written and compiled by
James Buckley, Jr. and David Fischer

CONTENTS

LONDON, NEW YORK, DELHI, MUNICH, and MELBOURNE

Project Editor Beth Sutinis
Art Editor Megan Clayton
Creative Director Tina Vaughan
Publisher Andrew Berkhut

Produced by
Shoreline Publishing Group LLC
Santa Barbara, California
Editorial Director James Buckley, Jr.
Designer Tom Carling, Carling Design, Inc.

Produced in partnership and licensed by
Major League Baseball Properties, Inc.
Executive Vice President Timothy J. Brosnan
Vice President of Publishing Don Hintze
Major League Baseball Properties, Inc.
245 Park Avenue, New York, New York 10167

First American Edition, 2002
02 03 04 05 2 4 6 8 10 9 7 5 3 1

Published in the United States by DK Publishing, Inc., 95 Madison Ave.
New York, New York 10016

Copyright © 2002 DK Publishing, Inc.
Text copyright © 2002 James Buckley, Jr.

DK Publishing, Inc. offers special discounts for bulk purchases for sales
promotions or premiums. Specific, large-quantity needs can be met
with special editions, including personalized covers, excerpts of
existing guides, and corporate imprints. For more information,
contact Special Markets Department, DK Publishing, Inc., 95
Madison Ave., New York, New York 10016

Library of Congress Cataloging-in-Publication Data

Baseball top 10

p. cm.

Summary: A compendium of more than two hundred twenty-five top
ten lists about baseball, covering such topics as most career strikeouts and
highest percentage of Hall of Fame votes received.

ISBN 0-7894-8506-0 (pbk.)

1.Baseball—Records—United States—Juvenile literature. 2. Baseball—
United States—History—Juvenile literature. [1. Baseball—Records.] I. Title:
Baseball top 10. II. Title: Baseball top ten.

GV877.4.M53 2002

796.357—dc21

2001047621

Reproduced by Colourscan, Singapore.
Printed and bound in the United States by R.R. Donnelly & Sons Co.

see our complete product line at
www.dk.com

TEAMS

GAMES

WORLD SERIES

BALLPARKS, FANS, AND MORE

Who's Number Ten?

You can probably name the player who has hit the most career home runs (if you can't, turn to page 10), or the pitcher with the most career victories (page 17). But can you name the player with the fifth-most homers? Or the 10th? Or the pitcher with the seventh-most wins? Well, this book is here to make sure that you can come up with those answers and hundreds more like them. By providing more than 225 top 10 lists of stats and trivia, *Baseball Top 10* proves that there is more to life—and baseball statistics—than coming in first.

If you're like most baseball fans, you're simply crazy for statistics. You absorb stats like a sponge sucks up water, and you spout them like a broken fountain. If that's you, then welcome to paradise. *Baseball Top 10* covers every part of the game—past and present, on and off the field, from the Majors to Little League. No matter what your favorite part of baseball is (or what your favorite team is), you'll find something in here that's right up your alley.

Where did we find this stuff?

We looked high and low (and everywhere in between) to find the names and numbers in this book. Our main source was Major League Baseball itself, of course, through their comprehensive Web site, *www.mlb.com*. The Elias Sports Bureau provides all the official stats for MLB, and this book reflects Elias's calculations and listings on the site. Another key source was the seventh edition of *Total Baseball* (Total/Sports Illustrated, 2001), the official encyclopedia of MLB. At more than 2,500 pages, it was invaluable to our search for baseball beyond Number One. More information about the sources is available on page 96. Also, note that the information in this edition of *Baseball Top 10*, including career totals for players and teams and World Series information, is completely updated through the 2001 postseason.

So, dig in. Have fun. Stump your friends and neighbors. We think you'll find a lot more than ten ways to enjoy *Baseball Top 10*.

PLAYERS

GOLDEN ARM

Rocket-armed catcher Ivan Rodriguez is one of several current players who have won multiple Gold Glove awards for fielding excellence.

MAJOR AWARDS

Most Cy Young Awards

PITCHER (SEASONS)	AWARDS
1 Roger Clemens (1986, '87, '91, '97, '98, 2001)	6
2= Steve Carlton (1972, '77, '80, '82)	4
= Greg Maddux (1992, '93, '94, '95)	4
= Randy Johnson (1995, '99, 2000, '01)	4
5= Pedro Martinez (1997, '99, 2000)	3
= Sandy Koufax (1963, '65, '66)	3
= Tom Seaver (1969, '73, '75)	3
= Jim Palmer (1973, '75, '76)	3

Five players are tied with 2 Cy Youngs

The Cy Young Award was given to one pitcher a year 1956–67, and to one pitcher from each league since then.

Recent Triple Crown Batters

	PLAYER (SEASON)	HR	RBI	BA
1	**Carl Yastrzemski** (1967)	44	121	.326
2	**Frank Robinson** (1966)	49	122	.316
3	**Mickey Mantle** (1956)	52	130	.353
4	**Ted Williams** (1947)	32	114	.343
5	**Ted Williams** (1942)	36	137	.356
6	**Joe Medwick** (1937)	31	154	.374
7	**Lou Gehrig** (1934)	49	165	.363
8=	**Chuck Klein** (1933)	28	120	.368
=	**Jimmie Foxx** (1933)	48	163	.356
10	**Rogers Hornsby** (1925)	39	143	.403

The batting Triple Crown—leading a league in home runs, runs batted in, and batting average—is one of baseball's rarest hitting feats.

THE MICK
Slugging outfielder Mickey Mantle of the Yankees combined speed and power like few others in baseball history. He is the all-time leader in home runs by a switch-hitter.

Top 10 Most Recent A.L. Cy Young Awards
(Pitcher/Season)

❶ **Roger Clemens**, 2001 ❷ **Pedro Martinez**, 2000 ❸ **Pedro Martinez**, 1999 ❹ **Roger Clemens**, 1998 ❺ **Roger Clemens**, 1997 ❻ **Pat Hentgen**, 1996 ❼ **Randy Johnson**, 1995 ❽ **David Cone**, 1994 ❾ **Jack McDowell**, 1993 ❿ **Dennis Eckersley**, 1992

Top 10 Most Recent N.L. Cy Young Awards
Pitcher/Season

❶ **Randy Johnson**, 2001 ❷ **Randy Johnson**, 2000 ❸ **Randy Johnson**, 1999 ❹ **Tom Glavine**, 1998 ❺ **Pedro Martinez**, 1997 ❻ **John Smoltz**, 1996 ❼ **Greg Maddux**, 1995 ❽ **Greg Maddux**, 1994 ❾ **Greg Maddux**, 1993 ❿ **Greg Maddux**, 1992

MARTINEZ MAGIC
In 1999, Pedro Martinez of the Red Sox became one of only three pitchers to win the Cy Young Award in each league. He is joined by Gaylord Perry and Randy Johnson in this elite club.

THE TOP 10

Recent A.L. Rookies of the Year

SEASON	PLAYER, TEAM
2001	**Ichiro Suzuki**, Seattle Mariners
2000	**Kazuhiro Sasaki**, Seattle Mariners
1999	**Carlos Beltran**, Kansas City Royals
1998	**Ben Grieve**, Oakland A's
1997	**Nomar Garciaparra**, Red Sox
1996	**Derek Jeter**, New York Yankees
1995	**Marty Cordova**, Minn. Twins
1994	**Bob Hamelin**, Kansas City Royals
1993	**Tim Salmon**, California Angels
1992	**Pat Listach**, Milwaukee Brewers

The Rookie of Year is also voted on by the BBWAA. The winner receives the Jackie Robinson Award, named for the great Dodgers' player who in 1947 became the first African-American player in the Majors in the 20th century. Robinson was named the rookie of the year that season while playing first base, though he later moved to second base.

THE TOP 10

Recent N.L. Rookies of the Year

SEASON	PLAYER, TEAM
2001	**Albert Pujols**, St. Louis Cardinals
2000	**Rafael Furcal**, Atlanta Braves
1999	**Scott Williamson**, Cin. Reds
1998	**Kerry Wood**, Chicago Cubs
1997	**Scott Rolen**, Philadelphia Phillies
1996	**Todd Hollandsworth**, Dodgers
1995	**Hideo Nomo**, Los Angeles Dodgers
1994	**Raul Mondesi**, Los Angeles Dodgers
1993	**Mike Piazza**, Los Angeles Dodgers
1992	**Eric Karros**, Los Angeles Dodgers

THE TOP 10

Recent N.L. MVPs

SEASON	PLAYER, TEAM
2001	**Barry Bonds**, San Francisco Giants
2000	**Jeff Kent**, San Francisco Giants
1999	**Chipper Jones**, Atlanta Braves
1998	**Sammy Sosa**, Chicago Cubs
1997	**Larry Walker**, Colorado Rockies
1996	**Ken Caminiti**, San Diego Padres
1995	**Barry Larkin**, Cincinnati Reds
1994	**Jeff Bagwell**, Houston Astros
1993	**Barry Bonds**, San Francisco Giants
1992	**Barry Bonds**, Pittsburgh Pirates

THE TOP 10

Recent A.L. MVPs

SEASON	PLAYER, TEAM
2001	**Ichiro Suzuki**, Seattle Mariners
2000	**Jason Giambi**, Oakland A's
1999	**Ivan Rodriguez**, Texas Rangers
1998	**Juan Gonzalez**, Texas Rangers
1997	**Ken Griffey, Jr.**, Seattle Mariners
1996	**Juan Gonzalez**, Texas Rangers
1995	**Mo Vaughn**, Boston Red Sox
1994	**Frank Thomas**, Chicago White Sox
1993	**Frank Thomas**, Chicago White Sox
1992	**Dennis Eckersley**, Oakland A's

QUIZ TIME
The single-season home run record is 73, set by Barry Bonds in 2001. But can you name the single-season record-holder for runs batted in? Answer on page 13.

9

HITTING STARS

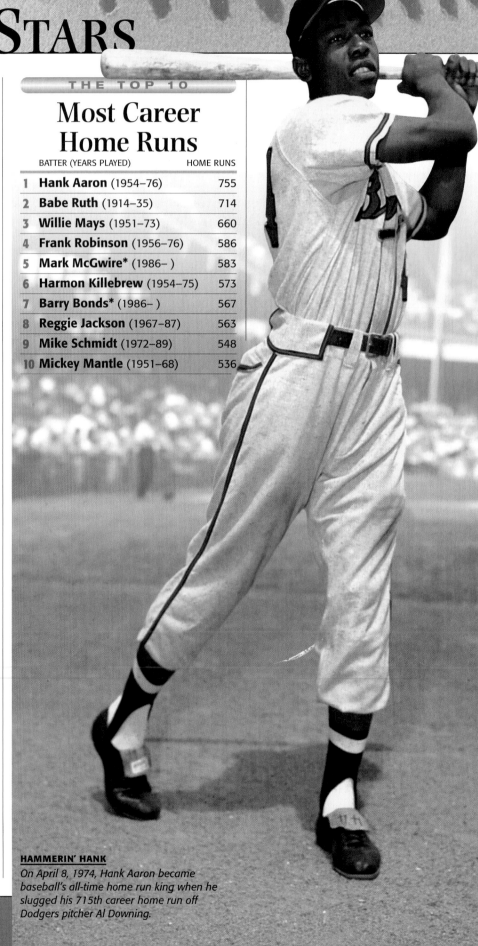

THE TOP 10

Most Career Hits

BATTER (YEARS PLAYED)	HITS
1 Pete Rose (1963–86)	4,256
2 Ty Cobb (1905–28)	4,189
3 Hank Aaron (1954–76)	3,771
4 Stan Musial (1941–63)	3,630
5 Tris Speaker (1907–28)	3,514
6 Honus Wagner (1897–1917)	3,420
7 Carl Yastrzemski (1961–83)	3,419
8 Paul Molitor (1978–98)	3,319
9 Eddie Collins (1906–30)	3,315
10 Willie Mays (1951–73)	3,283

Three thousand hits is the standard for hitting greatness combined with longevity. These ten players are the top of a list of only 25 who have reached that total in baseball history. The great Roberto Clemente made it onto that exclusive list with a double in the last at-bat of his great career, before he was tragically killed in an airplane crash in 1972. An interesting note: Cobb for many years was credited with 4,191 hits, but recent scholarly research has resulted in the new career total for him listed above.

THE TOP 10

Most Career Total Bases

BATTER (YEARS PLAYED)	TOTAL BASES
1 Hank Aaron (1954–76)	6,856
2 Stan Musial (1941–63)	6,134
3 Willie Mays (1951–73)	6,066
4 Ty Cobb (1905–28)	5,854
5 Babe Ruth (1914–35)	5,793
6 Pete Rose (1963–86)	5,752
7 Carl Yastrzemski (1961–83)	5,539
8 Eddie Murray (1977–97)	5,397
9 Frank Robinson (1956–76)	5,373
10 Dave Winfield (1973–95)	5,221

Total bases are calculated quite simply: by adding up the number of bases a player reaches via base hits. A single is one base, a double two, and so on.

THE TOP 10

Most Career Home Runs

BATTER (YEARS PLAYED)	HOME RUNS
1 Hank Aaron (1954–76)	755
2 Babe Ruth (1914–35)	714
3 Willie Mays (1951–73)	660
4 Frank Robinson (1956–76)	586
5 Mark McGwire* (1986–)	583
6 Harmon Killebrew (1954–75)	573
7 Barry Bonds* (1986–)	567
8 Reggie Jackson (1967–87)	563
9 Mike Schmidt (1972–89)	548
10 Mickey Mantle (1951–68)	536

HAMMERIN' HANK
On April 8, 1974, Hank Aaron became baseball's all-time home run king when he slugged his 715th career home run off Dodgers pitcher Al Downing.

THE TOP 10
Highest Career Batting Average

BATTER (YEARS PLAYED)	BATTING AVERAGE
1 **Ty Cobb** (1905–28)	.366
2 **Rogers Hornsby** (1915–37)	.358
3 **Joe Jackson** (1908–20)	.356
4 **Dan Brouthers** (1879–1904)	.349
5 **Pete Browning** (1882–94)	.349
6 **Ed Delahanty** (1888–1903)	.346
7 **Tris Speaker** (1907–28)	.345
8 **Billy Hamilton** (1888–1901)	.344
9 **Ted Williams** (1939–60)	.344
10 **Babe Ruth** (1914–35)	.342

For many years, Cobb's average was recorded as .367. But diligent research by amateur, and later, Major League experts revealed errors in the record books that dropped the mark by .001 (see top 10 list for career hits, too). But that does nothing to detract from Cobb's outstanding batting skill.

A note on batting average. You'll see several places where players with the same average are not listed as tied. That's because batting averages can be calculated beyond three digits as shown; the fourth digit can break the tie.

THE TOP 10
Longest Hitting Streak

BATTER (SEASON)	CONSECUTIVE GAMES
1 **Joe DiMaggio**, Yankees (1941)	56
2= **Willie Keeler**, Orioles (1897)	44
= **Pete Rose**, Reds (1978)	44
4 **Bill Dahlen**, Cubs (1894)	42
5 **George Sisler**, Browns (1922)	41
6 **Ty Cobb**, Tigers (1911)	40
7 **Paul Molitor**, Brewers (1987)	39
8 **Tommy Holmes**, Braves (1945)	37
9 **Billy Hamilton**, Phillies (1894)	36
10= **Fred Clarke**, Louisville (1895)	35
= **Ty Cobb**, Tigers (1917)	35

In the endless debate over what records are "unbreakable," DiMaggio's amazing streak often tops the list. Though he was certainly under enormous pressure during the 56 games that his streak comprised, one can only imagine the immense weight of media and fan interest that would pummel a player today who even approached that mark. Pete Rose tied the all-time National League mark in 1978 under a constant glare of publicity that, too, pales to today's media madness.

DYNAMIC DUO

Lou Gehrig and Babe Ruth combined to form baseball's most powerful slugging twosome. They dominated baseball in the 1920s and 1930s, helping the Yankees win four titles.

THE TOP 10
Highest Career Slugging Average

BATTER (YEARS PLAYED)	SLUGGING AVERAGE
1 **Babe Ruth** (1914–35)	.690
2 **Ted Williams** (1939–60)	.634
3 **Lou Gehrig** (1923–39)	.632
4 **Jimmie Foxx** (1925–45)	.609
5 **Hank Greenberg** (1930–47)	.605
6 **Manny Ramirez*** (1993–)	.594
7 **Mark McGwire*** (1986–)	.588
8 **Barry Bonds*** (1989–)	.585
9 **Mike Piazza*** (1992–)	.579
10 **Joe DiMaggio** (1936–51)	.579

Slugging average is calculated by dividing total bases by times at bat. A player who bats 50 times and has 30 total bases has a slugging average of .600. The number measures a player's ability to make extra-base hits, which are any hits except singles.

THE TOP 10
Most Career Runs Batted In

BATTER (YEARS PLAYED)	RUNS BATTED IN
1 **Hank Aaron** (1954–76)	2,297
2 **Babe Ruth** (1914–35)	2,213
3 **Lou Gehrig** (1923–39)	1,995
4 **Stan Musial** (1941–63)	1,951
5 **Ty Cobb** (1905–28)	1,938
6 **Jimmie Foxx** (1925–45)	1,922
7 **Eddie Murray** (1977–97)	1,917
8 **Willie Mays** (1951–73)	1,903
9 **Cap Anson** (1876–97)	1,880
10 **Mel Ott** (1926–47)	1,860

THE TOP 10
Most Runs Scored in a Career

BATTER (YEARS PLAYED)	RUNS SCORED
1 **Rickey Henderson*** (1979–28)	2,247
2 **Ty Cobb** (1905–28)	2,246
3 **Hank Aaron** (1954–76)	2,174
3 **Babe Ruth** (1914–35)	2,174
5 **Pete Rose** (1963–86)	2,165
6 **Willie Mays** (1951–73)	2,062
7 **Stan Musial** (1941–63)	1,949
8 **Lou Gehrig** (1923–39)	1,888
9 **Tris Speaker** (1907–28)	1,882
10 **Mel Ott** (1926–47)	1,859

* Active through 2001

QUIZ TIME
Rickey Henderson took over the all-time lead in runs scored in 2001. In what other major offensive category is Henderson also the career leader? Answer on page 15.

11

SINGLE-SEASON RECORDS

THE TOP 10

Highest Slugging Average in a Season

BATTER (SEASON)	SLUGGING AVERAGE
1 Barry Bonds* (2001)	.863
2 Babe Ruth (1920)	.847
3 Babe Ruth (1921)	.846
4 Babe Ruth (1927)	.772
5 Lou Gehrig (1927)	.765
6 Babe Ruth (1923)	.764
7 Rogers Hornsby (1925)	.756
8 Mark McGwire (1998)	.752
9 Jeff Bagwell (1994)	.750
10 Jimmie Foxx (1932)	.749

GOIN' YARD

Mark McGwire thrilled the sports world in 1998 with his pursuit of the single-season home run record. He obliterated the old mark of 61 with a stunning total of 70! But his record lasted only three seasons before Barry Bonds hit 73 in 2001.

Top Ten Total Bases in a Season

Batter (Season)/Total Bases

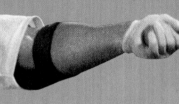

1 Babe Ruth (1921) 457 **2** Rogers Hornsby (1922) 450 **3** Lou Gehrig (1927) 447 **4** Chuck Klein (1930) 445 **5** Jimmie Foxx (1932) 438 **6** Stan Musial (1948) 429 **7** Sammy Sosa (2001) 425 **8** Hack Wilson (1930) 423 **9** Chuck Klein (1932) 420 **10** = Lou Gehrig (1930) 419; = Luis Gonzalez (2001) 419

THE TOP 10

Most Runs Scored in a Season

BATTER (SEASON)	RUNS SCORED
1 Billy Hamilton (1894)	198
2 = Tom Brown (1891)	177
= Babe Ruth (1921)	177
4 = Tip O'Neill (1887)	167
= Lou Gehrig (1936)	167
6 Billy Hamilton (1895)	166
7 = Willie Keeler (1894)	165
= Joe Kelley (1894)	165
9 = Arlie Latham (1887)	163
= Babe Ruth (1928)	163
= Lou Gehrig (1931)	163

THE TOP 10

Highest Batting Average in a Season

BATTER (SEASON)	BATTING AVERAGE
1 Tip O'Neill (1887)	.485
2 Pete Browning (1887)	.457
3 Bob Caruthers (1887)	.456
4 Hugh Duffy (1894)	.440
5 Yank Robinson (1887)	.427
6 Nap Lajoie (1901)	.426
7 Willie Keeler (1897)	.424
8 Rogers Hornsby (1924)	.424
9 Cap Anson (1887)	.421
10 Dan Brouthers (1887)	.420

DID YOU KNOW?

We don't have a list for lowest batting averages, but any player hitting under .200 is said to be hitting "below the Mendoza line," named for light-hitting shortstop Mario Mendoza.

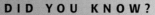

Most Hits in a Season

Batter (Season)/Hits

1 = **Pete Browning** (1887), 275; = **Tip O'Neill** (1887), 275 **3** **George Sisler** (1920), 257 **4** **Denny Lyons** (1887), 256 **5** = **Lefty O'Doul** (1929), 254; = **Bill Terry** (1930), 254 **7** **Al Simmons** (1925), 253 **8** **Oyster Burns** (1887), 251 **9** = **Rogers Hornsby** (1922), 250; = **Chuck Klein** (1930), 250

THE TOP 10

Most Runs Batted In in a Season

BATTER (SEASON)	RUNS BATTED IN
1 **Hack Wilson** (1930)	191
2 **Lou Gehrig** (1931)	184
3 **Hank Greenberg** (1937)	183
4 = **Lou Gehrig** (1927)	175
= **Jimmie Foxx** (1938)	175
6 **Lou Gehrig** (1930)	174
7 **Babe Ruth** (1921)	171
8 = **Chuck Klein** (1930)	170
= **Hank Greenberg** (1935)	170
10 **Jimmie Foxx** (1932)	169

THE TOP 10

Most Home Runs in a Season

BATTER (SEASON)	HOME RUNS
1 **Barry Bonds*** (2001)	73
2 **Mark McGwire*** (1998)	70
3 **Sammy Sosa*** (1998)	66
4 **Mark McGwire*** (1999)	65
5 **Sammy Sosa*** (2001)	64
6 **Sammy Sosa*** (1999)	63
7 **Roger Maris** (1961)	61
8 **Babe Ruth** (1927)	60
9 **Babe Ruth** (1921)	59
10 = **Mark McGwire** (1997)	58
= **Jimmie Foxx** (1932)	58
= **Hank Greenberg** (1938)	58

THE TOP 10

Highest OPS in a Season

BATTER (SEASON)	OPS
1 **Babe Ruth** (1920)	1.379
2 **Barry Bonds*** (2001)	1.378
3 **Babe Ruth** (1921)	1.359
4 **Babe Ruth** (1923)	1.309
5 **Ted Williams** (1941)	1.286
6 **Ted Williams** (1957)	1.259
7 **Babe Ruth** (1927)	1.258
8 **Babe Ruth** (1926)	1.253
9 **Babe Ruth** (1924)	1.252
10 = **Rogers Hornsby** (1925)	1.245

OPS is a fairly new addition to the list of statistics, and many experts feel it is the best measure of a player's overall hitting ability. OPS stands for on-base percentage plus slugging average. That is, it measures the two things a player must do well to excel: hit for average (i.e., get on base) and hit for power. Not surprisingly, Ruth again dominates this list. Barry Bonds's total of 1378 in his record-breaking 2001 season included a .515 on-base percentage, the highest in the Majors since 1957.

THE M&M BOYS

Thirty-seven years before Mark McGwire and Sammy Sosa created home run hysteria, a pair of New York Yankees did the same thing. In 1961, Roger Maris (left) and Mickey Mantle battled back and forth all summer long, with the pressure rising with each home run. In early September, with 54 home runs, Mantle fell seriously ill with an infection and had to sit out the rest of the season. Maris, though nearly overwhelmed with the attention, kept slugging, and on the last day of the season, hit his 61st home run, breaking Babe Ruth's record. At the time, he was criticized for doing it in 161 games to Ruth's 151, but the passage of time has earned Maris respect.

SNAP SHOTS

*Active through 2001

STREAKS AND STEALS

THE TOP 10

Most Consecutive Games Played

	PLAYER (YEARS OF STREAK)	GAMES
1	Cal Ripken, Jr. (1981–2001)	2,316
2	Lou Gehrig (1925–39)	2,130
3	Everett Scott (1916–25)	1,307
4	Steve Garvey (1974–83)	1,207
5	Billy Williams (1963–70)	1,117
6	Joe Sewell (1922–30)	1,103
7	Stan Musial (1951–57)	895
8	Eddie Yost (1949–55)	829
9	Gus Suhr (1932–38)	822
10	Nellie Fox (1952–59)	798

Ripken's pursuit of Gehrig's incredible streak was one of the biggest baseball stories of the 1990s. Both players not only racked up an amazing string of games while overcoming the dozens of daily injuries, aches, and pains that go along with playing baseball, but both excelled as players and as leaders off the field.

THE TOP 10

Career Games Played, All Time

	PLAYER (YEARS PLAYED)	GAMES
1	Pete Rose (1963–86)	3,562
2	Carl Yastrzemski (1961–83)	3,308
3	Hank Aaron (1954–76)	3,298
4	Ty Cobb (1905–28)	3,035
5	Eddie Murray (1977–97)	3,026
=	Stan Musial (1941–63)	3,026
7	Cal Ripken, Jr.* (1981–2001)	3,001
8	Willie Mays (1951–73)	2,992
9	Rickey Henderson* (1979–)	2,979
10	Dave Winfield (1973–95)	2,973

THE TOP 10

Most Consecutive Seasons Played with One Team

	PLAYER, TEAM	SEASONS
1=	Brooks Robinson, Orioles	23
=	Carl Yastrzemski, Red Sox	23
3=	Cap Anson, Cubs	22
=	Ty Cobb, Tigers	22
=	Al Kaline, Tigers	22
=	Stan Musial, Cardinals	22
=	Mel Ott, Giants	22
=	Henry Aaron, Braves	21
9=	George Brett, Royals	21
=	Harmon Killebrew, Senators/Twins	21
=	Willie Mays, Giants	21
=	Willie Stargell, Pirates	21
=	Cal Ripken, Jr.*, Orioles	21

With the advent of free agency and the increased player movement of recent decades, a player spending his entire career with one team has become more of a rarity, thus few players playing today have much real chance of cracking this list.

THE TOP 10

Career Games Played, Active

	PLAYER	SEASONS
1	Cal Ripken, Jr.	3,001
2	Rickey Henderson	2,979
3	Harold Baines	2,830
4	Tony Gwynn	2,440
5	Tim Raines	2,404
5	Barry Bonds	2,296
6	Rafael Palmeiro	2,258
7	Fred McGriff	2,201
9	Tony Fernandez	2,158
10	Bobby Bonilla	2,113

This list reflects players who completed the 2001 season. Future Hall-of-Famers Ripken and Gwynn retired after the 2001 season.

DID YOU KNOW?
The most surprising play in baseball is often the steal of home plate. Rod Carew of the Twins stole home seven times in 1969, tying Pete Reiser's single-season record.

THE TOP 10

Most Career Stolen Bases

	PLAYER (CAREER)	STOLEN BASES
1	**Rickey Henderson*** (1979–)	1,395
2	**Lou Brock** (1961–79)	938
3	**Billy Hamilton** (1888–1901)	914
4	**Ty Cobb** (1905–28)	892
5	**Tim Raines*** (1979–)	808
6	**Vince Coleman** (1985–97)	752
7	**Eddie Collins** (1906–30)	745
8	**Arlie Latham** (1880–1909)	742
9	**Max Carey** (1910–1929)	738
10	**Honus Wagner** (1897–1917)	723

IRON CAL

Cal Ripken, Jr., began his career as a third baseman, but later switched to shortstop, where he became a perennial All-Star. He later returned to third base, where he ended his career.

THE TOP 10

Highest Stolen Base Average in a Season

	BASERUNNER (SEASON)	STOLEN BASE AVERAGE
1=	**Kevin McReynolds** (1988)	100.0
=	**Paul Molitor** (1994)	100.0
3=	**Brady Anderson*** (1994)	96.9
=	**Carlos Beltran** (2001)	96.9
5	**Max Carey** (1922)	96.2
6	**Ken Griffey, Sr.** (1980)	95.8
7	**Stan Javier*** (1988)	95.2
8	**Doug Glanville*** (1999)	94.4
9	**Amos Otis** (1970)	94.3
10	**Jack Perconte** (1985)	93.9

Note that making this list required stealing a minimum of 20 bases in a season. McReynolds was not known as a speedster, but he made the most of his attempts, being successful on 21 of 21 in 1988. Molitor stole 504 bases in his great career, including 20 for 20 in 1994. Pirates and Dodgers outfielder Max Carey is another all-time great in stolen bases, with 738 for his career.

THE TOP 10

Highest Career Stolen Base Average

	PLAYER (YEARS PLAYED)	STOLEN BASE AVERAGE
1	**Tony Womack*** (1993–)	85.3
2	**Tim Raines*** (1979–)	84.6
3	**Eric Davis*** (1984–)	84.0
4	**Henry Cotto** (1984–93)	83.3
5	**Barry Larkin*** (1986–)	83.2
5	**Willie Wilson** (1976–94)	83.3
7	**Davey Lopes** (1972–87)	83.0
8	**Stan Javier*** (1984–)	82.8
9	**Julio Cruz** (1977–1986)	81.5
10	**Joe Morgan** (1963–1984)	81.0

This statistic is calculated by dividing the number of stolen bases by the number of stolen base attempts. Successful basestealers combine speed, timing, and careful study of pitchers' pickoff moves.

THE TOP 10

Most Stolen Bases in a Season

	PLAYER (SEASON)	STOLEN BASES
1	**Hugh Nicol** (1887)	138
2	**Rickey Henderson** (1982)	130
3	**Arlie Latham** (1887)	129
4	**Lou Brock** (1974)	118
5	**Charlie Comiskey** (1887)	117
6=	**John Ward** (1887)	111
=	**Billy Hamilton** (1889)	111
=	**Billy Hamilton** (1891)	111
9	**Vince Coleman** (1985)	110
10=	**Arlie Latham** (1888)	109
=	**Vince Coleman** (1987)	109

Rickey Henderson's 130 steals in 1982, the most in almost 100 years, is regarded as the modern Major League record.

THE IRON HORSE

Before Cal Ripken proved that unbreakable records can indeed be broken, Yankees first baseman Lou Gehrig was the standard by which all other "iron men" were judged. He stepped in for an ailing Wally Pipp in 1925 and didn't give up the job for 14 seasons. Among baseball's greatest all-time sluggers, Gehrig was almost universally liked by teammates and opponents. Thus when he was struck down by amyotrophic lateral sclerosis (ALS), a muscular and nervous system disease, the entire baseball world was saddened. The disease ended his career in 1939 and his life in 1941.

SNAP SHOTS

*Active through 2001.

PITCHING ACES

Career Games Pitched

PITCHER (YEARS PLAYED)	GAMES
1 Jesse Orosco* (1979–)	1,131
2 Dennis Eckersley (1975–98)	1,071
3 Hoyt Wilhelm (1952–72)	1,070
4 Kent Tekulve (1974–89)	1,050
5 Lee Smith (1980–97)	1,022
6 Rich Gossage (1972–94)	1,002
7 John Franco* (1984–)	998
8 Lindy McDaniel (1955–75)	987
9 Dan Plesac* (1986–)	946
10 Rollie Fingers (1965–85)	944

UNBREAKABLE?

Cy Young averaged more than 23 wins per season during his 21-year career. Of course, he's also the all-time leader in losses with 316.

ROCKET MAN

Roger Clemens of the New York Yankees became the all-time leader for strikeouts in the American League during the 2001 season.

DID YOU KNOW?

In 1972, Philadelphia's Steve Carlton won 27 games (and the Cy Young Award). His Phillies won only 59 games. It was the highest-ever percentage of team wins by one pitcher.

THE TOP 10

Shutouts in a Career

	PITCHER (YEARS PLAYED)	SHUTOUTS
1	**Walter Johnson** (1907–27)	110
2	**Pete Alexander** (1911–30)	90
3	**Christy Mathewson** (1900–16)	79
4	**Cy Young** (1890–1911)	76
5	**Eddie Plank** (1901–17)	69
6	**Warren Spahn** (1942–65)	63
7=	**Nolan Ryan** (1966–93)	61
=	**Tom Seaver** (1967–86)	61
9	**Bert Blyleven** (1970–92)	60
10	**Don Sutton** (1966–88)	58

A shutout is earned when a pitcher wins an official, complete game and the other team does not score a run.

THE TOP 10

Career Saves

	PITCHER (YEARS PLAYED)	SAVES
1	**Lee Smith** (1980–97)	478
2	**John Franco*** (1984–)	422
3	**Dennis Eckersley** (1975–98)	390
4	**Jeff Reardon** (1979–94)	367
5	**Randy Myers** (1985–98)	347
6	**Rollie Fingers** (1968–85)	341
7	**John Wetteland** (1989–2000)	330
8	**Rick Aguilera** (1985–2000)	318
9	**Trevor Hoffman*** (1993–)	314
10	**Tom Henke** (1982–95)	311

A save is normally awarded to a pitcher who enters the game with the winning runs on deck, at the plate, or on the bases, and who then finishes the game without the other team tying the game or taking a lead. Notice that these top 10 leaders in saves all played after 1970, when the role of the relief pitcher began to be more prominent. By the early 1980s, each team usually had one "closer," who pitched only the ninth inning of games or a little more, resulting in increases in the number of saves awarded.

THE TOP 10

Career Wins

	PITCHER (YEARS PLAYED)	WINS
1	**Cy Young** (1890–1911)	511
2	**Walter Johnson** (1907–27)	417
3=	**Pete Alexander** (1911–30)	373
=	**Christy Mathewson** (1900–16)	373
5	**Warren Spahn** (1942–65)	363
6=	**Jim Galvin** (1875–92)	361
=	**Kid Nichols** (1890–1906)	361
8	**Tim Keefe** (1880–93)	342
9	**Steve Carlton** (1965–88)	329
10	**John Clarkson** (1882–94)	328

THE TOP 10

Career Strikeouts by Pitcher

	PITCHER (YEARS PLAYED)	STRIKEOUTS
1	**Nolan Ryan** (1966–93)	5,714
2	**Steve Carlton** (1965–88)	4,136
3	**Roger Clemens*** (1984–)	3,717
4	**Bert Blyleven** (1970–92)	3,701
5	**Tom Seaver** (1967–86)	3,640
6	**Don Sutton** (1966–88)	3,574
7	**Gaylord Perry** (1962–83)	3,534
8	**Walter Johnson** (1904–24)	3,508
9	**Randy Johnson** (1988–)	3,412
10	**Phil Niekro** (1964–87)	3,342

THE TOP 10

Career Earned Run Average (ERA)

	PITCHER (YEARS PLAYED)	ERA
1	**Ed Walsh** (1904–17)	1.82
2	**Addie Joss** (1902–10)	1.89
3	**Mordecai Brown** (1903–16)	2.06
4	**John M. Ward** (1878–84)	2.10
5	**Christy Mathewson** (1900–16)	2.13
6	**Rube Waddell** (1897–1910)	2.16
7	**Walter Johnson** (1907–27)	2.17
8	**Orval Overall** (1905–10, 1913)	2.23
9	**Tommy Bond** (1874–84)	2.25
10	**Ed Reulbach** (1905–17)	2.28

Earned run average is calculated by multiplying a pitcher's earned runs by 9, then dividing the result by the number of innings pitched. An earned run is charged to a pitcher as long as an error did not help the run score or the runner who scored to reach base.

Mordecai Brown was known as "Three Fingered." Brown earned his nickname the hard way, by losing a finger and parts of two others in a boyhood farming accident. He may have gained by the loss, however, as the movement on his fastball caused by his unusual hand may have helped him achieve success.

THE RYAN EXPRESS

Nolan Ryan threw longer than any pitcher in Major League history, and possibly harder. He began his career with an overpowering fastball, but he was never sure where it was going. He was as famous for his wildness as his 100-mph heater. As he matured as a pitcher, he combined power with precision. In 1973, he set the single-season record with 383 strikeouts. Ryan threw 7 no-hitters, more than any other pitcher.

SNAP SHOTS

PITCHING ACES

THE TOP 10

Most Wins in a Season

PITCHER (SEASON)	WINS
1 **Charley Radbourn** (1884)	59
2 **John Clarkson** (1885)	53
3 **Guy Hecker** (1884)	52
4 **John Clarkson** (1889)	49
5=**Charley Radbourn** (1883)	48
=**Charlie Buffinton** (1884)	48
7=**Al Spalding** (1876)	47
=**John Ward** (1879)	47
9=**Jim Galvin** (1883)	46
=**Jim Galvin** (1884)	46
=**Matt Kilroy** (1887)	46

All these pitchers played before the "modern" era; the list below shows most victories in a season since 1900. Many of the pitchers above threw with the then-mandatory underhand motion.

THE TOP 10

Most Strikeouts in a Season

PITCHER (SEASON)	STRIKEOUTS
1 **Matt Kilroy** (1886)	513
2 **Toad Ramsey** (1886)	499
3 **Hugh Daily** (1884)	483
4 **Dupee Shaw** (1884)	451
5 **Charley Radbourn** (1884)	441
6 **Charlie Buffinton** (1884)	417
7 **Guy Hecker** (1884)	385
8 **Nolan Ryan** (1973)	383
9 **Sandy Koufax** (1965)	382
10 **Bill Sweeney** (1884)	374

Again, comparisons of pre-1900s play with modern play are skewed by the huge difference in appearances by early pitchers. But note that Ryan and Koufax's totals were piled up in far fewer games, yet still approach all-time single-season bests. Ryan's 383 is the modern record.

THE TOP 10

Most Strikeouts per Nine Innings in a Season

PITCHER (SEASON)	STRIKEOUTS
1 **Randy Johnson** (2001)	13.44
2 **Pedro Martinez** (1999)	13.20
3 **Kerry Wood** (1998)	12.58
4 **Randy Johnson** (2000)	12.56
5 **Randy Johnson** (1995)	12.35
6 **Randy Johnson** (1997)	12.30
7 **Randy Johnson** (1998)	12.12
8 **Randy Johnson** (1999)	12.06
9 **Pedro Martinez** (2000)	11.78
10 **Nolan Ryan** (1987)	11.48

Calculated by dividing a pitcher's innings by nine, to equal a full game, and then dividing that number into total strikeouts in a season, this is a great measure of a power pitcher's overpowering nature.

THE TOP 10

Most Wins in a Season Since 1900

PITCHER (SEASON)	WINS
1 **Jack Chesbro** (1904)	41
2 **Ed Walsh** (1908)	40
3 **Christy Mathewson** (1908)	37
4 **Joe McGinnity** (1904)	35
5 **Joe Wood** (1912)	34
6=**Cy Young** (1901)	33
=**Christy Mathewson** (1904)	33
=**Walter Johnson** (1912)	33
=**Grover Alexander** (1916)	33
=Four players tied with	32

The only pitcher to win 30 games in a season since 1935 was Denny McLain of Detroit, who went 31–6 in 1968, a year in which pitchers dominated.

THE TOP 10

Most Walks Allowed in a Career

PITCHER (SEASONS PLAYED)	WALKS
1 **Nolan Ryan** (1966–93)	2,795
2 **Steve Carlton** (1965–88)	1,833
3 **Phil Niekro** (1964–87)	1,809
4 **Early Wynn** (1939–63)	1,775
5 **Bob Feller** (1936–56)	1,764
6 **Bobo Newsom** (1929–53)	1,732
7 **Amos Rusie** (1889–1901)	1,707
8 **Charlie Hough** (1970–94)	1,665
9 **Gus Weyhing** (1887–1901)	1,570
10 **Red Ruffing** (1924–47)	1,541

For much of his career, Ryan was as well known for his wildness as his startling speed. He threw seven no-hitters, but never had a perfect game, thanks to walks.

THE TOP 10

Lowest Earned Run Average in a Season

PITCHER (SEASON)	ERA
1 **Tim Keefe** (1880)	0.86
2 **Dutch Leonard** (1914)	0.96
3 **Mordecai Brown** (1906)	1.04
4 **Bob Gibson** (1968)	1.12
5 **Christy Mathewson** (1909)	1.14
6 **Walter Johnson** (1913)	1.14
7 **Jack Pfiester** (1907)	1.15
8 **Addie Joss** (1908)	1.16
9 **Carl Lundgren** (1907)	1.17
10 **Denny Driscoll** (1882)	1.21

Gibson's 1968 mark stands out as the lowest in recent years. That season was called the "Year of the Pitcher," when hitting stats were at an all-time low.

DID YOU KNOW?
Four balls equal a walk, right? Not until 1889, though. Before then, the number of balls for a walk (or base on balls) was as high as nine, before shrinking to today's number.

Top 10 Most Saves in a Season

Pitcher (Season)/Saves

❶ Bobby Thigpen (1990), 57 **❷ = Randy Myers** (1993), 53; **= Trevor Hoffman** (1998), 53 **❹ Dennis Eckersley** (1992), 51; **= Rod Beck** (1998), 51 **❻ Mariano Rivera** (2001), 50 **❼ = Dennis Eckersley** (1990), 48; **= Rod Beck** (1993), 48; **= Jeff Shaw** (1998), 48 **❿ Lee Smith** (1991), 47

SUPER SAVER
In 18 seasons with eight teams, Lee Smith has nine seasons with 30 or more saves and led his league in saves four times.

Most Losses in a Career

PITCHER (SEASONS PLAYED)	LOSSES
1 **Cy Young** (1890–1911)	316
2 **Jim Galvin** (1875–92)	308
3 **Nolan Ryan** (1966–93)	292
4 **Walter Johnson** (1907–27)	279
5 **Phil Niekro** (1964–87)	274
6 **Gaylord Perry** (1962–83)	265
7 **Don Sutton** (1966–88)	256
8 **Jack Powell** (1897–1912)	254
9 **Eppa Rixey** (1912–33)	251
10 **Bert Blyleven** (1970–92)	250

The old saying is that you've got to be pretty good to pitch long enough to lose this often. Notice that all-time "loser" Cy Young also holds the record for most career wins.

Most Games Pitched in a Season

PITCHER (SEASON)	GAMES
1 **Mike Marshall** (1974)	106
2 **Kent Tekulve** (1979)	94
3 **Mike Marshall** (1973)	92
4 **Kent Tekulve** (1978)	91
5 = **Wayne Granger** (1969)	90
= **Mike Marshall** (1979)	90
= **Kent Tekulve** (1987)	90
8 = **Mark Eichhorn** (1987)	89
= **Julian Tavarez** (1997)	89
= **Steve Kline** (2001)	89
11 = **Wilbur Wood** (1968)	88
= **Mike Myers** (1997)	88
= **Sean Runyan** (1998)	88

Marshall was legendary for his fitness and preparation, and later wrote books on training and workouts for pitchers.

FIELDING ARTISTS

GOLD GLOVE

This photo is of Willie Mays's 1962 Rawlings Gold Glove. Since 1957, baseball writers have voted for the top fielders at each position. The size of this glove would be amazing to early fielders, who used tiny gloves or no gloves at all. The improvement in equipment and training in recent years has meant that many of the top all-time fielders played in recent seasons.

SNAP SHOTS

THE TOP 10
Career Fielding Average, Third Base

	FIELDER (SEASONS PLAYED)	FIELDING AVERAGE
1	Brooks Robinson (1955–77)	.971
2	Ken Reitz (1972–82)	.970
3	George Kell (1943–57)	.969
4=	Steve Buechele (1985–95)	.968
5=	Don Money (1968–83)	.968
6=	Don Wert (1963–71)	.968
7=	Willie Kamm (1923–35)	.967
8=	Heinie Groh (1912–27)	.967
9=	Travis Fryman* (1990–)	.966
10	Carney Lansford (1978–92)	.966

THE TOP 10
Career Fielding Average, First Base

	FIELDER (SEASONS PLAYED)	FIELDING AVERAGE
1	Steve Garvey (1969–87)	.996
2	Don Mattingly (1982–95)	.996
3	Wes Parker (1964–72)	.996
4	J.T. Snow* (1992–)	.996
5	Dan Driessen (1973–87)	.995
6	David Segui* (1990–)	.995
7	John Olerud* (1989–)	.995
8	Jim Spencer (1968–82)	.995
9	Tino Martinez* (1990–)	.995
10	Mark Grace* (1988–)	.995

THE TOP 10
Career Fielding Average, Shortstop

	FIELDER (SEASONS PLAYED)	FIELDING AVERAGE
1	Omar Vizquel* (1989–)	.983
2	Mike Bordick* (1990–)	.981
3	Larry Bowa (1970–85)	.980
4	Tony Fernandez* (1983–)	.980
5	Cal Ripken, Jr.* (1981–)	.979
6	Ozzie Smith (1978–96)	.978
7	Spike Owen (1983–95)	.977
8	Alan Trammell (1977–96)	.977
9	Mark Belanger (1965–82)	.977
10	Bucky Dent (1973–84)	.976

THE TOP 10
Career Fielding Average, Second Base

	FIELDER (SEASONS PLAYED)	FIELDING AVERAGE
1	Ryne Sandberg (1981–97)	.989
2	Tom Herr (1979–91)	.989
3	Mickey Morandini* (1990–)	.989
4	Jose Lind (1987–95)	.988
5	Jody Reed (1987–97)	.988
6	Bret Boone* (1992–)	.986
7	Jim Gantner (1976–92)	.985
8	Craig Biggio* (1988–)	.985
9	Frank White (1973–90)	.984
10	Bobby Grich (1970–86)	.984

Sandberg was not only the best fielder at his position, per this list, but he was also one of the top-hitting "keystone" men ever.

THE TOP 10
Career Fielding Average, Outfield

	FIELDER (SEASONS PLAYED)	FIELDING AVERAGE
1	Darryl Hamilton* (1988–)	.995
2	Darren Lewis* (1990–)	.994
3	Terry Puhl (1977–91)	.993
4	Brett Butler (1981–97)	.993
5	Pete Rose (1963–86)	.991
6	Amos Otis (1967–84)	.991
7	Joe Rudi (1967–82)	.991
8	Mickey Stanley (1964–78)	.991
9	Tom Goodwin (1991–)	.991
10	Robin Yount (1974–93)	.990

DID YOU KNOW?
Fielding average is calculated by adding putouts and assists and dividing that total by the total of putouts, assists, and errors. The fewer errors you make, the higher your average.

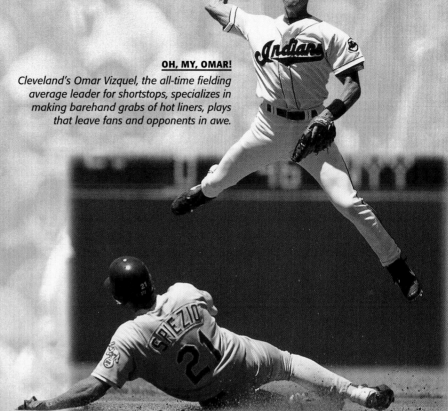

Career Fielding Average, Pitcher

FIELDER (SEASONS PLAYED)	FIELDING AVERAGE
1 **Don Mossi** (1954–65)	.990
2 **Gary Nolan** (1967–77)	.990
3 **Rick Rhoden** (1974–89)	.989
4 **Lon Warneke** (1930–45)	.988
5 **Jim Wilson** (1945–58)	.988
6 **Woodie Fryman** (1966–83)	.988
7 **Larry Gura** (1970–85)	.986
8 **Mike Mussina***(1991–)	.985
9 **Grover Alexander** (1911–30)	.985
10 **Alvin Crowder** (1926–36)	.984

A good-fielding pitcher can really help himself out by becoming a fifth infielder. Mussina is not only one of the A.L.'s top pitchers, he has won four Gold Gloves. Since ending his baseball career, Rhoden has become a professional golfer, winning consistently on a celebrity pro tour.

OH, MY, OMAR!

Cleveland's Omar Vizquel, the all-time fielding average leader for shortstops, specializes in making barehand grabs of hot liners, plays that leave fans and opponents in awe.

HUMAN VACUUM CLEANER

Baltimore third baseman Brooks Robinson set a new standard for excellence at the hot corner over his 23-year career. He almost singlehandedly won the 1970 World Series with several game-saving plays at third base, including this diving grab.

Career Fielding Average, Catcher

FIELDER (SEASONS PLAYED)	FIELDING AVERAGE
1 **Bill Freehan** (1961–76)	.993
2 **Elston Howard** (1955–68)	.993
3 **Jim Sundberg** (1974–89)	.993
4 **Sherm Lollar** (1946–63)	.992
5 **Mike Macfarlane** (1987–99)	.992
6 **Johnny Edwards** (1961–74)	.992
7 **Tom Haller** (1961–72)	.992
8 **Lance Parrish** (1977–95)	.991
9 **Jerry Grote** (1963–81)	.991
10 **Ernie Whitt** (1976–91)	.991

GOLD GLOVES

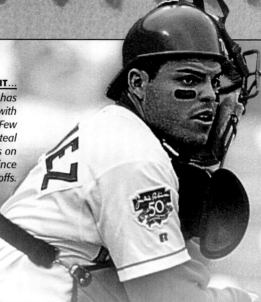

The lists on these two pages show the ten most recent winners of the Rawlings Gold Glove award for each position. Gold Gloves are given to one player in each league at each infield position, while three awards are given in each league for outfielders. Individual awards for right-, center-, and leftfield are not given; all outfielders are lumped together. Players earn these awards by subjective voting, not by strict statistical measures.

GO AHEAD, TRY IT...
Texas catcher Ivan Rodriguez has redefined the catching position with his remarkable throwing arm. Few baserunners even attempt to steal on him anymore, while runners on first need to be on their toes, since he's equally adept at pickoffs.

THE TOP 10
Most Recent Catchers

N.L. WINNER	YEAR	A.L. WINNER
Brad Ausmus, Houston	**2001**	**Ivan Rodriguez**, Texas
Mike Matheny, St. Louis	**2000**	**Ivan Rodriguez**, Texas
Mike Lieberthal, Phil.	**1999**	**Ivan Rodriguez**, Texas
Charles Johnson, Fla.-L.A.	**1998**	**Ivan Rodriguez**, Texas
Charles Johnson, Florida	**1997**	**Ivan Rodriguez**, Texas
Charles Johnson, Florida	**1996**	**Ivan Rodriguez**, Texas
Charles Johnson, Florida	**1995**	**Ivan Rodriguez**, Texas
Tom Pagnozzi, St. Louis	**1994**	**Ivan Rodriguez**, Texas
Kirt Manwaring, S.F.	**1993**	**Ivan Rodriguez**, Texas
Tom Pagnozzi, St. Louis	**1992**	**Ivan Rodriguez**, Texas

THE TOP 10
Most Recent First Basemen

N.L. WINNER	YEAR	A.L. WINNER
Todd Helton, Colorado	**2001**	**Doug Mientkiewicz**, Minn.
J.T. Snow, S.F.	**2000**	**John Olerud**, Seattle
J.T. Snow, S.F.	**1999**	**Rafael Palmeiro**, Texas
J.T. Snow, S.F.	**1998**	**Rafael Palmeiro**, Baltimore
J.T. Snow, S.F.	**1997**	**Rafael Palmeiro**, Baltimore
Mark Grace, Chicago	**1996**	**J.T. Snow**, California
Mark Grace, Chicago	**1995**	**J.T. Snow**, California
Jeff Bagwell, Houston	**1994**	**Don Mattingly**, New York
Mark Grace, Chicago	**1993**	**Don Mattingly**, New York
Mark Grace, Chicago	**1992**	**Don Mattingly**, New York

THE TOP 10
Most Recent Pitchers

N.L. WINNER	YEAR	A.L. WINNER
Greg Maddux, Atlanta	**2001**	**Mike Mussina**, New York
Greg Maddux, Atlanta	**2000**	**Kenny Rogers**, Texas
Greg Maddux, Atlanta	**1999**	**Mike Mussina**, Baltimore
Greg Maddux, Atlanta	**1998**	**Mike Mussina**, Baltimore
Greg Maddux, Atlanta	**1997**	**Mike Mussina**, Baltimore
Greg Maddux, Atlanta	**1996**	**Mike Mussina**, Baltimore
Greg Maddux, Atlanta	**1995**	**Mark Langston**, California
Greg Maddux, Atlanta	**1994**	**Mark Langston**, California
Greg Maddux, Atlanta	**1993**	**Mark Langston**, California
Greg Maddux, Chicago	**1992**	**Mark Langston**, California

THE TOP 10
Most Recent Second Basemen

N.L. WINNER	YEAR	A.L. WINNER
Fernando Viña, St. Louis	**2001**	**Roberto Alomar**, Cleveland
Pokey Reese, Cincinnati	**2000**	**Roberto Alomar**, Cleveland
Pokey Reese, Cincinnati	**1999**	**Roberto Alomar**, Cleveland
Bret Boone, Cincinnati	**1998**	**Roberto Alomar**, Baltimore
Craig Biggio, Houston	**1997**	**Chuck Knoblauch**, Minnesota
Craig Biggio, Houston	**1996**	**Roberto Alomar**, Toronto
Craig Biggio, Houston	**1995**	**Roberto Alomar**, Toronto
Craig Biggio, Houston	**1994**	**Roberto Alomar**, Toronto
Robby Thompson, S.F.	**1993**	**Roberto Alomar**, Toronto
Jose Lind, Pittsburgh	**1992**	**Roberto Alomar**, Toronto

QUIZ TIME
What rare Gold Glove feat did outfielder Jim Edmonds accomplish in 2000? Hint: In 2000, he joined the St. Louis Cardinals. (Answer on page 26.)

THE TOP 10

Most Recent Third Basemen

N.L. WINNER	YEAR	A.L. WINNER
Scott Rolen, Philadelphia	**2001**	**Eric Chavez**, Oakland
Scott Rolen, Philadelphia	**2000**	**Travis Fryman**, Cleveland
Robin Ventura, New York	**1999**	**Scott Brosius**, New York
Scott Rolen, Philadelphia	**1998**	**Robin Ventura**, Chicago
Ken Caminiti, San Diego	**1997**	**Matt Williams**, Cleveland
Ken Caminiti, San Diego	**1996**	**Robin Ventura**, Chicago
Ken Caminiti, San Diego	**1995**	**Wade Boggs**, New York
Matt Williams, S.F.	**1994**	**Wade Boggs**, New York
Matt Williams, S.F.	**1993**	**Robin Ventura**, Chicago
Terry Pendleton, Atlanta	**1992**	**Robin Ventura**, Chicago

THE TOP 10

Most Recent Shortstops

N.L. WINNER	YEAR	A.L. WINNER
Orlando Cabrera, Montreal	**2001**	**Omar Vizquel**, Cleveland
Neifi Perez, Colorado	**2000**	**Omar Vizquel**, Cleveland
Rey Ordoñez, New York	**1999**	**Omar Vizquel**, Cleveland
Rey Ordoñez, New York	**1998**	**Omar Vizquel**, Cleveland
Rey Ordoñez, New York	**1997**	**Omar Vizquel**, Cleveland
Barry Larkin, Cincinnati	**1996**	**Omar Vizquel**, Cleveland
Barry Larkin, Cincinnati	**1995**	**Omar Vizquel**, Cleveland
Barry Larkin, Cincinnati	**1994**	**Omar Vizquel**, Cleveland
Jay Bell, Pittsburgh	**1993**	**Omar Vizquel**, Seattle
Ozzie Smith, St. Louis	**1992**	**Cal Ripken, Jr.**, Baltimore

THE TOP 10

Most Recent Outfielders

N.L. WINNERS	YEAR	A.L. WINNERS
Andruw Jones, Atlanta **Larry Walker**, Colorado **Jim Edmonds**, St. Louis	**2001**	**Ichiro Suzuki**, Seattle **Mike Cameron**, Seattle **Torii Hunter**, Minnesota
Andruw Jones, Atlanta **Steve Finley**, Arizona **Jim Edmonds**, St. Louis	**2000**	**Darin Erstad**, Anaheim **Bernie Williams**, New York **Jermaine Dye**, Kansas City
Andruw Jones, Atlanta **Steve Finley**, Arizona **Larry Walker**, Colorado	**1999**	**Ken Griffey, Jr.**, Seattle **Shawn Green**, Toronto **Bernie Williams**, New York
Barry Bonds, S.F. **Andruw Jones**, Atlanta **Larry Walker**, Colorado	**1998**	**Jim Edmonds**, Anaheim **Ken Griffey, Jr.**, Seattle **Bernie Williams**, New York
Barry Bonds, S.F. **Raul Mondesi**, Los Angeles **Larry Walker**, Colorado	**1997**	**Jim Edmonds**, Anaheim **Ken Griffey, Jr.**, Seattle **Bernie Williams**, New York
Barry Bonds, S.F. **Marquis Grissom**, Atlanta **Steve Finley**, San Diego	**1996**	**Ken Griffey, Jr.**, Seattle **Kenny Lofton**, Cleveland **Jay Buhner**, Seattle
Barry Bonds, S.F. **Marquis Grissom**, Atlanta **Steve Finley**, San Diego	**1995**	**Ken Griffey, Jr.**, Seattle **Kenny Lofton**, Cleveland **Devon White**, Toronto
Barry Bonds, S.F. **Darren Lewis**, S.F. **Marquis Grissom**, Montreal	**1994**	**Ken Griffey, Jr.**, Seattle **Devon White**, Toronto **Kenny Lofton**, Cleveland
Barry Bonds, S.F. **Larry Walker**, Colorado **Marquis Grissom**, Montreal	**1993**	**Ken Griffey, Jr.**, Seattle **Devon White**, Toronto **Kenny Lofton**, Cleveland
Barry Bonds, S.F. **Larry Walker**, Colorado **Andy Van Slyke**, Pittsburgh	**1992**	**Ken Griffey, Jr.**, Seattle **Devon White**, Toronto **Kirby Puckett**, Minnesota

YOUNG GLOVE

Atlanta centerfielder Andruw Jones is not only the first Major Leaguer from Curaçao, but he's one of the top young fielders in the game.

GOLD GLOVES

Most Gold Gloves, Pitcher

PITCHER	GOLD GLOVES
1 Jim Kaat	16
2 Greg Maddux*	12
3= Bob Gibson	9
= Bobby Shantz	8
5 Mark Langston	7
6= Phil Niekro	6
= Ron Guidry	6
8 Mike Mussina*	5
8 Jim Palmer	4
10 Harvey Haddix	3

Although he was 6'4" and weighed more than 200 pounds, Jim "Kitty" Kaat (pronounced "KAHT") is generally regarded as the best-fielding pitcher ever. His 16 Gold Gloves attest to that. But he was a pretty fair pitcher, too, winning 283 games in his career with a lifetime 3.45 ERA.

Most Gold Gloves, Catcher

CATCHER	GOLD GLOVES
1= Johnny Bench	10
= Ivan Rodriguez	10
3 Bob Boone	7
4 Jim Sundberg	6
5 Bill Freehan	5
6= Del Crandall	4
= Charles Johnson	4
= Tony Peña	4
9= Seven players tied with	3

"THE CATCH"

To make the most famous catch in baseball history, Willie Mays had to track down Vic Wertz's drive on a dead run and with his back to the plate. The catch came, dramatically, in Game 1 of the 1954 World Series.

Most Gold Gloves, First Base

FIRST BASEMAN	GOLD GLOVES
1 Keith Hernandez	11
2 Don Mattingly	9
3 George Scott	8
4= Vic Power	7
= Bill White	7
6= Wes Parker	6
= J.T. Snow*	6
8= Steve Garvey	4
= Mark Grace*	4
10= Gil Hodges	3
= Eddie Murray	3
= Rafael Palmeiro*	3
= Joe Pepitone	3

Most Gold Gloves, Second Base

SECOND BASEMAN	GOLD GLOVES
1= Roberto Alomar*	10
2 Ryne Sandberg	9
3= Bill Mazeroski	8
= Frank White	8
5= Joe Morgan	5
= Bobby Richardson	5
7= Craig Biggio*	4
= Bobby Grich	4
9= Nellie Fox	3
= Davey Johnson	3
= Bobby Knoop	3
= Harold Reynolds	3
= Manny Trillo	3
= Lou Whitaker	3

DID YOU KNOW?
In 1957, Gold Gloves were given to one player from each outfield position: Willie Mays in center, Al Kaline in right, and Minnie Minoso in left.

Most Gold Gloves, Third Base

THIRD BASEMAN	GOLD GLOVES
1 Brooks Robinson	16
2 Mike Schmidt	10
3= Buddy Bell	6
= Robin Ventura*	6
5= Ken Boyer	5
= Doug Rader	5
= Ron Santo	5
8= Gary Gaetti	4
= Matt Williams*	4
10= Ken Caminiti*	3
= Frank Malzone	3
= Terry Pendleton	3
= Tim Wallach	3
= Scott Rolen	3

Most Gold Gloves, Shortstop

SHORTSTOP	GOLD GLOVES
1 Ozzie Smith	13
2 Luis Aparicio	9
= Omar Vizquel*	9
4= Mark Belanger	8
5 Dave Concepcion	5
6= Tony Fernandez*	4
= Alan Trammell	4
8= Barry Larkin	3
= Roy McMillan	3
= Rey Ordoñez*	3

The Wizard of Oz set the standard for shortstops during his 19-year career with the Padres and Cardinals. Current Indians shortstop Omar Vizquel might be approaching Ozzie's status, however.

Most Gold Gloves, Outfield

OUTFIELDER	GOLD GLOVES
1= Roberto Clemente	12
= Willie Mays	12
3= Ken Griffey, Jr.*	10
= Al Kaline	10
5= Paul Blair	8
= Barry Bonds*	8
= Andre Dawson	8
= Dwight Evans	8
= Garry Maddox	8
10= Curt Flood	7
= Devon White	7
= Dave Winfield	7
= Carl Yastrzemski	7

Most Consecutive Gold Gloves, Any Position

PLAYER, POSITION	CONSEC. GGs
1= Jim Kaat, P	16
= Brooks Robinson, 3B	16
3 Ozzie Smith, SS	13
4= Willie Mays, OF	12
= Roberto Clemente, OF	12
= Greg Maddux*, P	12
7= Keith Hernandez, 1B	11
8= Johnny Bench, C	10
= Ivan Rodriguez*, C	10
= Ken Griffey, Jr.*, OF	10
10= Bob Gibson, P	9
= Ryne Sandberg, 2B	9
= Omar Vizquel, SS	9

Active through 2001.

ASSISTS AND PUTOUTS

Top 10 Career Assists, Third Base
Player/Assists

1 **Brooks Robinson**, 6,205 **2** **Graig Nettles**, 5,279
3 **Mike Schmidt**, 5,045 **4** **Buddy Bell**, 4,925
5 **Ron Santo**, 4,581 **6** **Gary Gaetti**, 4,531
7 **Eddie Mathews**, 4,322 **8** **Wade Boggs**, 4,246
9 **Aurelio Rodriguez**, 4,150 **10** **Ron Cey**, 4,018

Top 10 Most Assists in a Season, Third Base
Player (Season) Assists

1 **Graig Nettles** (1971) 412 **2** = **Graig Nettles** (1973) 410; =
Brooks Robinson (1974) 410 **4** = **Harlond Clift** (1937) 405;
= **Brooks Robinson** (1967) 405 **6** **Mike Schmidt** (1974) 404
7 **Doug DeCinces** (1982) 399 **8** = **Clete Boyer** (1962) 396;
= **Mike Schmidt** (1977) 396; = **Buddy Bell** (1982) 396

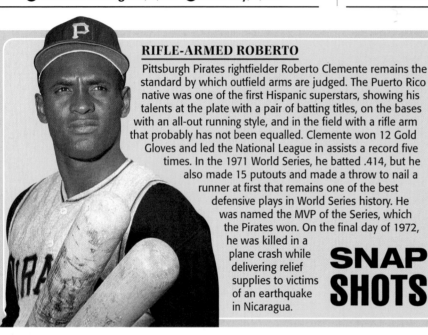

RIFLE-ARMED ROBERTO

Pittsburgh Pirates rightfielder Roberto Clemente remains the standard by which outfield arms are judged. The Puerto Rico native was one of the first Hispanic superstars, showing his talents at the plate with a pair of batting titles, on the bases with an all-out running style, and in the field with a rifle arm that probably has not been equalled. Clemente won 12 Gold Gloves and led the National League in assists a record five times. In the 1971 World Series, he batted .414, but he also made 15 putouts and made a throw to nail a runner at first that remains one of the best defensive plays in World Series history. He was named the MVP of the Series, which the Pirates won. On the final day of 1972, he was killed in a plane crash while delivering relief supplies to victims of an earthquake in Nicaragua.

THE TOP 10
Most Career Assists, Shortstop

PLAYER (SEASONS PLAYED)	ASSISTS
1 **Ozzie Smith** (1978–96)	8,375
2 **Luis Aparicio** (1956–73)	8,016
3 **Bill Dahlen** (1891–1911)	7,505
4 **Rabbit Maranville** (1912–35)	7,354
5 **Luke Appling** (1930–50)	7,218
6 **Tommy Corcoran** (1890–1907)	7,110
7 **Cal Ripken, Jr.*** (1981–)	6,977
8 **Larry Bowa** (1970–85)	6,857
9 **Dave Concepcion** (1970–88)	6,594
10 **Dave Bancroft** (1915–30)	6,561

THE TOP 10
Most Career Assists, Catcher

PLAYER (SEASONS PLAYED)	ASSISTS
1 **Deacon McGuire** (1884–1912)	1,860
2 **Ray Schalk** (1912–29)	1,811
3 **Steve O'Neill** (1911–28)	1,698
4 **Red Dooin** (1902–16)	1,590
5 **Chief Zimmer** (1884–1903)	1,580
6 **Johnny Kling** (1900–13)	1,554
7 **Ivey Wingo** (1911–29)	1,487
8 **Wilbert Robinson** (1886–1902)	1,454
9 **Bill Bergen** (1901–11)	1,444
10 **Wally Schang** (1913–31)	1,420

THE TOP 10
Most Assists in a Season, Catcher

PLAYER (SEASON)	ASSISTS
1 **Bill Rariden** (1915)	238
2 **Bill Rariden** (1914)	215
3 **Pat Moran** (1903)	214
4 = **Oscar Stanage** (1911)	212
= **Art Wilson** (1914)	212
6 **Gabby Street** (1909)	210
7 **Frank Snyder** (1915)	204
8 **George Gibson** (1910)	203
9 = **Bill Bergen** (1909)	202
= **Claude Berry** (1914)	202

THE TOP 10
Most Assists in a Season, Shortstop

PLAYER (SEASON)	ASSISTS
1 **Ozzie Smith** (1980)	621
2 **Glenn Wright** (1924)	601
3 **Dave Bancroft** (1920)	598
4 **Tommy Thevenow** (1926)	597
5 **Ivan DeJesus** (1977)	595
6 **Cal Ripken** (1984)	583
7 **Whitey Wietelmann** (1943)	581
8 **Dave Bancroft** (1922)	579
9 **Rabbit Maranville** (1914)	574
10 **Don Kessinger** (1968)	573

* Active through 2001

DID YOU KNOW?
Putout: When a player tags the base or the player to make an out. Assist: A throw to a player who makes a putout. (Page 22 answer: Edmonds won Gold Gloves in both leagues.)

THE TOP 10

Most Career Assists, Second Base

	PLAYER (SEASONS PLAYED)	ASSISTS
1	**Eddie Collins** (1906–30)	7,630
2	**Charlie Gehringer** (1924–42)	7,068
3	**Joe Morgan** (1963–84)	6,967
4	**Bid McPhee** (1882–99)	6,915
5	**Bill Mazeroski** (1956–72)	6,685
6	**Lou Whitaker** (1977–95)	6,653
7	**Nellie Fox** (1947–65)	6,373
8	**Ryne Sandberg** (1981–97)	6,363
9	**Willie Randolph** (1975–92)	6,336
10	**Napoleon Lajoie** (1896–1916)	6,262

THE TOP 10

Most Assists in a Season, Second Base

	PLAYER (SEASON)	ASSISTS
1	**Frankie Frisch** (1927)	641
2	**Hughie Critz** (1926)	588
3	**Rogers Hornsby** (1927)	582
4	**Ski Melillo** (1930)	572
5	**Ryne Sandberg** (1983)	571
6	**Rabbit Maranville** (1924)	568
7	**Frank Parkinson** (1922)	562
8	**Tony Cuccinello** (1936)	559
9	**Johnny Hodapp** (1930)	557
10	**Lou Bierbauer** (1892)	555

BILLY BUCKS

Though unfortunately remembered for an error in Game 6 of the seven-game 1986 World Series, Bill Buckner was one of the game's top-fielding first basemen throughout his career.

THE TOP 10

Most Career Assists, First Base

	PLAYER (SEASONS PLAYED)	PUTOUTS
1	**Eddie Murray** (1888–1907)	1,865
2	**Keith Hernandez** (1907–21)	1,682
3	**Mark Grace*** (1977–)	1,601
4	**George Sisler** (1871–97)	1,529
5	**Wally Joyner** (1916–36)	1,452
6	**Mickey Vernon** (1909–27)	1,448
7	**Fred Tenney** (1939–60)	1,363
8	**Bill Buckner** (1910–24)	1,351
=	**Chris Chambliss** (1914)	1,351
10	**Norm Cash** (1930–47)	1,317

First basemen who put up good assists numbers are generally the better fielders. A first baseman who can contribute in ways other than just catching infielders' throws can significantly improve a team's defense.

THE TOP 10

Most Putouts in a Season, First Base

	PLAYER (SEASON)	PUTOUTS
1	**Jiggs Donahue** (1907)	1,846
2	**George Kelly** (1920)	1,759
3	**Phil Todt** (1926)	1,755
4	**Wally Pipp** (1926)	1,710
5	**Jiggs Donahue** (1906)	1,697
6	**Candy LaChance** (1904)	1,691
7	**Tom Jones** (1907)	1,687
8	**Ernie Banks** (1965)	1,682
9	**Wally Pipp** (1922)	1,667
10	**Lou Gehrig** (1927)	1,662

First basemen don't rack up as many assists as other fielders. Their main job is cleanly catching throws from infielders to make outs at first base. They also earn putouts by catching ground balls and tagging first base, or by catching fly balls or line drives.

MISCELLANEOUS STATS

Grounded into Most Double Plays

	PLAYER (SEASONS PLAYED)	GIDPS
1	Hank Aaron (1954–76)	328
2	Carl Yastrzemski (1960–83)	323
3	Dave Winfield (1974–89)	319
4	Eddie Murray (1977–97)	316
5	Jim Rice (1974–89)	315
6	Cal Ripken, Jr. (1981–2001)	302
7=	Rusty Staub (1963–85)	297
=	Brooks Robinson (1955–77)	297
9	Ted Simmons (1968–88)	287
10	Joe Torre (1960–77)	284

This list is dominated by slow, righthanded sluggers who often pulled the ball.

Most Recent Unassisted Triple Plays

	PLAYER, POSITION	YEAR
1	Randy Velarde*, 2B	2000
2	John Valentin*, SS	1994
3	Mickey Morandini*, 2B	1992
4	Ron Hansen, SS	1968
5	Johnny Neun, 1B	1927
6	Jimmy Cooney, SS	1927
7	Glenn Wright, SS	1925
8	Ernie Padgett, SS	1923
9	George Burns, 1B	1923
10	Bill Wambsganss, 2B	1920

A fielder making three putouts by himself on one batted ball is the rarest fielding feat.

Most Batters Hit by Pitchers

	PITCHER	HBPs
1	Gus Weyhing	278
2	Chick Frasier	219
3	Pink Hawley	210
3	Walter Johnson	205
5	Eddie Plank	190
6	Tony Mullane	185
7	Joe McGinnity	179
8	Charlie Hough	174
9	Clark Griffith	171
10	Cy Young	163

With one of the best fastballs of all time, Walter Johnson had a fearsome weapon to use. He also wasn't afraid to throw inside, and not everyone got out of the way.

MY THREE VICTIMS

Bill Wambsganss, left, poses with the three players he got out in his 1920 triple play: Clarence Mitchell, Pete Kilduff, and Otto Miller.

THE TOP 10

Best 2B/SS Double-Play Combination in a Season

YEAR, 2ND BASEMAN/SHORTSTOP (DPS), TEAM — TOTAL DPS

		TOTAL DPS
1	1966, **Bill Mazeroski** (161), **Gene Alley** (128), Pitt.	289
2	1950, **Gerry Priddy** (150), **Johnny Lipon** (126), Det.	276
3	1962, **Bill Mazeroski** (138), **Dick Groat** (126), Pitt.	264
4	1949, **Bobby Doerr** (134), **Vern Stephens** (128), Bos.	262
5	1961, **Bill Mazeroski** (144), **Dick Groat** (117), Pitt.	261
6=	1950, **Jerry Coleman** (137), **Phil Rizzuto** (123), NYY	260
=	1966, **Bobby Knoop** (135), **Jim Fregosi** (125), Cal.	260
8	1928, **Hughie Critz** (124), **Hod Ford** (128), Cin.	252
9	1954, **Johnny Temple** (117), **Roy McMillan** (129), Cin.	246
10=	1943, **Ray Mack** (123), **Lou Boudreau** (122), Cleve.	245
=	1950, **Bobby Doerr** (130), **Vern Stephens** (115), Bos.	245
=	1958, **Bill Mazeroski** (118), **Dick Groat** (127), Pitt.	245
=	1974, **Dave Cash** (141), **Larry Bowa** (104), Phi.	245

When he was inducted into the Baseball Hall of Fame in 2001, Bill Mazeroski thanked voters for recognizing defense. "Maz" earned his selection mostly on the strength of his great glove.

PHILADELPHIA FLINGER
Robin Roberts of the Phillies enjoys a place in the Hall of Fame, but he doesn't enjoy his all-time record for most home runs allowed.

THE TOP 10

Most Times Hit by Pitch, Career

	PITCHER	HBPs
1	**Don Baylor**	267
2	**Ron Hunt**	243
3	**Frank Robinson**	198
3	**Craig Biggio***	197
5	**Minnie Miñoso**	192
6	**Andres Galarraga***	166
7	**Brady Anderson***	152
8	**Chet Lemon**	151
9	**Carlton Fisk**	143
10	**Nellie Fox**	142

Until he was overtaken by power-hitting Don Baylor, Expos outfielder Ron Hunt set the standard for being plunked by pitches. In 1971, Hunt was hit by pitches 50 times, the most ever in one season.

THE TOP 10

Most Home Runs Allowed, Single-season

PITCHER, SEASON — HRS

	PITCHER, SEASON	HRS
1	**Bert Blyleven**, 1986	50
2	**Jose Lima***, 2000	48
3=	**Robin Roberts**, 1956	46
=	**Bert Blyleven**, 1987	46
5	**Pedro Ramos**, 1957	43
6	**Denny McLain**, 1966	42
7	**Robin Roberts**, 1955	41
=	**Phil Niekro**, 1979	41
=	**Rick Helling**, 1999	41
10	Nine tied with	40

Blyleven must have been doing something right between giving up all those dingers. In 1986, he also won 17 games for the Twins.

THE TOP 10

Most Career Home Runs Allowed

	PITCHER	HRS
1	**Robin Roberts**	505
2	**Ferguson Jenkins**	484
3	**Phil Niekro**	482
4	**Don Sutton**	472
5	**Frank Tanana**	448
6	**Warren Spahn**	434
7	**Bert Blyleven**	430
8	**Steve Carlton**	414
9	**Gaylord Perry**	399
10	**Jim Kaat**	395

* Active through 2001

QUIZ TIME
You can probably guess that Ty Cobb is the all-time best hitter among outfielders. But can you name the second baseman with the highest career average? See page 30.

THE TOP 10

All-Time Hitters, Pitchers

PITCHERS	CAREER BATTING AVERAGE
1 Babe Ruth	.299
2 Guy Hecker	.297
3 Jack Stivetts	.295
4 Jim Devlin	.293
5 Charlie Ferguson	.288
6 George Uhle	.286
7 Wes Ferrell	.284
8 Charlie Sweeney	.284
9 Cy Seymour	.280
10 Doc Crandall	.279

Before the designated hitter came along in the American League in 1973, all pitchers took their regular turns at bat. In the National League, they still do. Pitchers rarely are great hitters; they don't practice hitting often and they only play every four or five days. However, many are good athletes who may have batted more often when younger.

THE RAJAH
Cardinals second baseman Rogers Hornsby batted .424 in 1922, the second-highest of the century. No player has topped that mark since.

THE TOP 10

All-Time Hitters, Shortstops

PLAYER	CAREER BATTING AVERAGE
1 Honus Wagner	.328
2 Arky Vaughan	.318
3 Joe Sewell	.312
4 Luke Appling	.310
5 Ed McKean	.308
6 Joe Cronin	.301
7 Barry Larkin	.299
8 Lou Boudreau	.295
9 George Davis	.295
10 Jack Glasscock	.294

THE TOP 10

All-Time Hitters, First Basemen

PLAYER	CAREER BATTING AVERAGE
1 Dan Brouthers	.349
2 Bill Terry	.341
3 George Sisler	.340
4 Lou Gehrig	.340
5 Cap Anson	.333
6 Rod Carew	.328
7 Jimmie Foxx	.325
8 Roger Connor	.323
9 Frank Thomas	.319
10 Hank Greenberg	.313

"Big" Dan Brouthers won five batting titles in his career, which stretched from 1879–1896. He was also one of baseball's early sluggers, with a .519 career slugging average that was the highest of any player in the 19th century.

THE TOP 10

All-Time Hitters, Second Basemen

PLAYER	CAREER BATTING AVERAGE
1 Rogers Hornsby	.358
2 Nap Lajoie	.338
3 Eddie Collins	.333
4 Charlie Gehringer	.320
5 Frankie Frisch	.316
6 Jackie Robinson	.311
7 Cupid Childs	.306
8 Billy Herman	.304
9 Roberto Alomar*	.306
10 Buddy Myer	.303

Lajoie hit over .300 in 16 of his 21 seasons and his .426 average in 1901 is the highest ever in the American League. Along with his skills as batter, Eddie Collins led his league in fielding nine times, plus twice stole a record six bases in one game.

THE TOP 10

All-Time Hitters, Third Basemen

PLAYER	CAREER BATTING AVERAGE
1 Wade Boggs	.328
2 Pie Traynor	.320
3 Denny Lyons	.318
4 Frank Baker	.307
5 George Kell	.306
6 George Brett	.305
7 Bill Madlock	.305
8 Stan Hack	.301
9 Pinky Whitney	.295
10 Kevin Seitzer	.295

Boggs and catcher Mike Piazza are the only recent player atop one of these positional lists. Boggs batted above .300 14 times and had at least 200 hits in seven seasons. He rarely hit for power but was one of baseball's consistently successful hitters.

QUIZ TIME
What fireballing righthander received the most votes of any pitcher in 1999 balloting for Major League Baseball's All-Century Team? (See page 33.)

THE TOP 10

All-Time Hitters, Catchers

PLAYER	CAREER BATTING AVERAGE
1 Mike Piazza*	.325
2 Mickey Cochrane	.320
3 Bill Dickey	.313
4 Spud Davis	.308
5 Ernie Lombardi	.306
6 Ivan Rodriguez*	.304
7 Gabby Hartnett	.297
8 Manny Sanguillen	.296
9 Smoky Burgess	.295
10 Thurman Munson	.292

AS EASY AS PIAZZA PIE

Mike Piazza has put up better numbers for home runs, RBI, and average in his first nine seasons than any catcher in the Hall of Fame. He is the best hitter ever to play baseball's most demanding position.

THE TOP 10

All-Time Hitters, Outfielders

PLAYER	CAREER BATTING AVERAGE
1 Ty Cobb	.366
2 Joe Jackson	.356
3 Ed Delahanty	.346
4 Tris Speaker	.345
5 Billy Hamilton	.344
6 Ted Williams	.344
7 Babe Ruth	.342
8 Harry Heilmann	.342
9 Willie Keeler	.341
10 Tony Gwynn*	.338

* Active through 2001

HISTORY'S BEST

Most Hall-of-Fame Votes Received

	PLAYER	VOTES
1	Nolan Ryan	491
2	George Brett	488
3	Mike Schmidt	444
4	Steve Carlton	436
5	Dave Winfield	435
6	Johnny Bench	431
7	Tom Seaver	425
8=	Kirby Puckett	423
=	Carl Yastrzemski	423
10	Jim Palmer	411

THE TOP 10

First 10 Negro League Players in the Hall of Fame

	PLAYER/POSITION	YEAR ELECTED
1	Satchel Paige/Pitcher	1971
2=	Josh Gibson/Catcher	1972
=	Buck Leonard/First Base	1972
4	Monte Irvin/Outfield	1973
5	Cool Papa Bell/Outfield	1974
6	Judy Johnson/Third Base	1975
7	Oscar Charleston/Outfield	1976
8=	Martin Dihigo/Pitcher-Outfield	1977
=	Pop Lloyd/Shortstop-First Base	1977
10	Rube Foster/Pitcher-Manager	1982

To make up for the past injustices that kept black ballplayers out of the Major Leagues, a special commission was set up in 1971 to select players from the Negro Leagues deemed worthy of induction in the Hall based on their career skills and achievements. The committee inducted nine players and disbanded in 1977. Through 2001, a total of 24 players from Negro League teams have been inducted.

A CLASSY CLASS
A gathering of greats in 1939: (top) Honus Wagner, Pete Alexander, Tris Speaker, Nap Lajoie, George Sisler, Walter Johnson; (bottom) Eddie Collins, Babe Ruth, Connie Mack, Cy Young.

The First 10 Players Elected to the Hall of Fame
Players/Year Elected

❶ Ty Cobb, Babe Ruth, Honus Wagner, Christy Mathewson, Walter Johnson, 1936 **❷ Nap Lajoie, Tris Speaker, Cy Young, George Wright,** 1937 **❸ Grover Alexander, George Sisler, Eddie Collins, Willie Keeler,** 1939

Okay, twelve. So sue us. These were the members of the first three player classes elected to the Baseball Hall of Fame. In addition, the following non-players were elected in these first three years: Managers John McGraw and Connie Mack, executives Ban Johnson and Morgan Bulkeley, and innovators Alexander Cartwright and Henry Chadwick.

THE TOP 10

Most Recent Hall-of-Fame Classes

YEAR	INDUCTEES
2001	Kirby Puckett, Dave Winfield, Bill Mazeroski, Hilton Smith
2000	Sparky Anderson, Carlton Fisk, Bid McPhee, Tony Perez, Turkey Stearnes
1999	George Brett, Orlando Cepeda, Nestor Chylak, Nolan Ryan, Frank Selee, Smokey Joe Williams, Robin Yount
1998	George Davis, Larry Doby, Lee McPhail, Joe Rogan, Don Sutton
1997	Nellie Fox, Tom Lasorda, Phil Niekro, Willie Wells
1996	Jim Bunning, Bill Foster, Ned Hanlon, Earl Weaver
1995	Richie Ashburn, Leon Day, William Hulbert, Mike Schmidt, Vic Willis
1994	Steve Carlton, Leo Durocher, Phil Rizzuto
1993	Reggie Jackson
1992	Rollie Fingers, Bill McGowan, Hal Newhouser, Tom Seaver

New members of the Hall are announced each January, with induction ceremonies held at Cooperstown, New York, each July or August.

QUIZ TIME
Which of the great Negro League Hall of Famers listed here is the all-time leader in Negro League batting average? Hint: He didn't play in the outfield. See page 34 for the answer.

Highest Percentages of Hall of Fame votes received

	PLAYER (INDUCTION YEAR)	PCT.
1	**Tom Seaver** (1992)	98.80
2	**Nolan Ryan** (1999)	98.79
3	**Ty Cobb** (1936)	98.20
4	**George Brett** (1999)	98.19
5	**Hank Aaron** (1982)	97.80
6	**Mike Schmidt** (1995)	98.2
7	**Johnny Bench** (1989)	96.40
8	**Steve Carlton** (1994)	96.40
9=	**Honus Wagner** (1936)	95.10
=	**Babe Ruth** (1936)	95.10

Most members of the Baseball Hall of Fame are selected by the Baseball Writers Association of America's special panel of electors. In addition, there are special committees to elect players who played more than 15 years ago (Veterans' Committee), Negro League players, executives, and others. A person must be named on 75 percent of the ballots of his electors to be inducted; electors may select more than one player per year.

All-Century Team Most Votes, Fan Ballots

	PLAYER, POSITION	VOTES
1	Lou Gehrig, 1B	1,207,992
2	Babe Ruth, OF	1,158,044
3	Henry Aaron, OF	1,156,782
4	Ted Williams, OF	1,125,583
5	Willie Mays, OF	1,115,896
6	Joe DiMaggio, OF	1,054,423
7	Johnny Bench, C	1,010,403
8	Nolan Ryan, RHP	992,040
9	Mickey Mantle, OF	988,168
10	Sandy Koufax, LHP	970,434

In 1999, fans and baseball experts selected the 30-member All-Century Team to honor the greatest players in baseball history. Two players were chosen at every infield position, along with nine pitchers and nine outfielders. These players received the highest numbers of total votes.

JUST PERFECT

Sandy Koufax, a member of MLB's All-Century team, is congratulated by teammates following his 1965 perfect game.

WHY COOPERSTOWN?

Why is the Baseball Hall of Fame in Cooperstown, New York? Good question. In 1905, sporting goods magnate Albert Spalding tried to find out who had "invented" baseball. A letter claimed that Union Army General Abner Doubleday "invented" baseball one day in 1839. One problem: Doubleday never was in Cooperstown and didn't invent baseball. Nevertheless, the little town became the "home" of the game, and the Hall was opened there in 1939. Scholars have traced baseball's roots back to the 1840s and earlier, but baseball didn't have a single "inventor."

SNAP SHOTS

"Total Player" Ratings*

	PLAYER	RATING
1	**Babe Ruth**	108.9
2	**Willie Mays**	95.9
3	**Nap Lajoie**	95.5
4	**Ty Cobb**	92.0
5	**Barry Bonds***	89.4
6	**Hank Aaron**	89.1
7	**Tris Speaker**	88.2
8	**Ted Williams**	83.0
9	**Rogers Hornsby**	82.7
10	**Honus Wagner**	81.8

Total Baseball is the official encyclopedia of Major League Baseball. Published every two seasons by Total Sports/Sports Illustrated, the book includes the writers' own unique "Total Player" ranking of all players. Total Player rankings are derived from a complicated formula that takes into account the average performances of a player's time, his "replacement value" to his team, and of course his career statistics. All of that data somehow translates into the numbers listed above. Trust us. (*Through 2000.)

* Active through 2001

OL' SATCH

How good was Satchel Paige? According to legend, he would often send his fielders to the dugout during exhibition games…and then strike out the side.

THE TOP 10

All-Time Negro League Pitchers

	PLAYER	WINS
1	Satchel Paige	143
2	Joe Rogan	109
3	Nip Winters	89
4=	Bill Drake	83
=	Bill Foster	79
6	Webster McDonald	65
7=	Chet Brewer	51
=	Ted Radcliffe	49

Holway's book lists only the top eight pitchers, ranked by pitching wins. These career numbers might seem low in comparison to Major League totals, but the Negro League season was shorter, and organized leagues were not around for as many years. However, all these pitchers played in many exhibition games along with organized league games. Ted "Double Duty" Radcliffe gained fame and a great nickname by pitching one end of a doubleheader and catching the other.

The Top Ten All-Time Negro League Batters
Player/Batting Average

1 Josh Gibson, .379 **2** Chino Smith, .375 **3** Jud Wilson, .370 **4** = Dobie Moore, .359; = Dewey Creacy, .359 **6** Willie Wells, .358; **7** = Oscar Charleston, .353; = Valentin Dreke, .353 **9** Turkey Stearnes, .352 **10** Cool Papa Bell, .343

Negro League stats are famously incomplete and hard to track down. Thanks to John Holway's "Blackball Stars" for these Negro League historical lists.

POWER MAN

Slugging catcher Josh Gibson was, according to some, the greatest hitter of all time in any league. Some historians credit him with more homers than Ruth or Aaron.

THE TOP 10

Federal League Teams

TEAM	TOTAL PCT.
1 Indianapolis*	.575
2 Chicago	.560
3 Newark*	.526
4 Pittsburgh	.495
5 Buffalo	.493
6 St. Louis	.488
7 Kansas City	.486
8 Brooklyn	.480
9 Baltimore	.417

(*Played only one season.) Since 1900, the only rival to the A.L. and N.L. has been the Federal League, formed in 1914. Nine teams (they are ranked here by their two-year Federal League winning percentages) played for two seasons before the league broke up and the players returned to their former teams.

THE TOP 10

Most Recent AAGBL Champions

TEAM	YEAR
1 Kalamazoo Lassies	1954
2 Grand Rapids Chicks	1953
3 South Bend Blue Sox	1952
4 South Bend Blue Sox	1951
5 Rockford Peaches	1950
6 Rockford Peaches	1949
7 Rockford Peaches	1948
8 Grand Rapids Chicks	1947
9 Racine Belles	1946
10 Rockford Peaches	1945

THE TOP 10

Most Recent AAGBL Players of the Year

PLAYER, TEAM	YEAR
1 Joanne Weaver, Fort Wayne	1954
2 Jean Faut, South Bend	1953
3 Betty Foss, Fort Wayne	1952
4 Jean Faut, South Bend	1951
5 Alma Ziegler, Grand Rapids	1950
6 Doris Sams, Muskegon	1949
7 Audrey Wagner, Kenosha	1948
8 Doris Sams, Muskegon	1947
9 Sophie Kurys, Racine	1946
10 Connie Wisniewski, Grd. Rapids	1945

During World War II, entrepreneur Philip Wrigley, owner of the Chicago Cubs, created the All-American Girls Professional Baseball League to entertain fans missing the male players off fighting the war. The league began by playing fast-pitch softball but evolved into real baseball. The league was formed in 1943 and disbanded in 1954.

THE TOP 10

First National Association Teams

TEAM	YEAR
1 Philadelphia Athletics	1871
2 Chicago White Stockings	1871
3 Boston Red Stockings	1871
4 Washington Olympics	1871
5 New York Mutuals	1871
6 Troy Haymakers	1871
7 Fort Wayne Kekiongas	1871
8 Cleveland Forest Citys	1871
9 Rockford Forest Citys	1871

The National Association existed from 1871–75. Some historians date the beginning of the Major Leagues to this league. This list reflects the order of finish in the N.A.'s first season. Two teams were added in 1872; by 1875, there were 13.

THE PLAYERS LEAGUE

One of the most remarkable and versatile individuals in baseball history was also partly responsible for one of the early challenges to the dominance of the Major Leagues. John Montgomery Ward was a league-leading pitcher for Providence of the National League; he pitched the second-ever perfect game in 1880. He later became a star shortstop with the New York Giants and a top basestealer. After earning a law degree in 1885 while still playing, he became involved in baseball labor issues and helped form the first "union," the Brotherhood of Professional Base Ball Players. In 1890, after their demands went unmet, dozens of players left their teams to form the Players League. Eight teams were formed, with Ward joining Brooklyn. But the Players League disbanded after only one season and the players went back to their former teams. Ward was elected to the Hall of Fame in 1964.

SNAP SHOTS

QUIZ TIME

Help in a pinch: What player holds the Major League record for most career pinch hits?
Hint: He set the record in 2001. See page 36.

35

BUNTS & PINCHES

Most Career Pinch Hits

	PLAYER (SEASONS PLAYED)	PINCH HITS
1	Lenny Harris* (1988–)	151
2	Manny Mota (1962–82)	150
3	Smoky Burgess (1949–67)	145
4	Greg Gross (1973–89)	143
5	Jose Morales (1973–84)	123
6	John Vander Wal* (1991–)	117
7	Jerry Lynch (1954–66)	116
8	Red Lucas (1923–38)	114
9	Steve Braun (1971–85)	113
10	Dave Hansen* (1990–)	110

Successful pinch hitting has become a specialized skill. Players take the place of teammates at the plate in an effort to jump-start a team's offense.

Best Career Pinch Hitting Avg.*

	PLAYER (SEASONS PLAYED)	BATTING AVERAGE
1	Alex Arias* (1992–)	.322
2	Tommy Davis (1959–76)	.320
3	Frenchy Bordagaray (1934–45)	.312
4	Frankie Baumholtz (1947–57)	.307
5	Willie McGee (1982–99)	.307
6	Sid Bream (1983–94)	.306
7	Mark Carreon (1987–96)	.306
8	Red Schoendienst (1945–63)	.303
9	Bob Fothergill (1922–33)	.300
10	Dave Philley (1941–62)	.299

*minimum 150 at-bats

THE TOP 10

Most Pinch Hit Home Runs

PLAYER (SEASONS PLAYED)	HOME RUNS
1 **Cliff Johnson** (1972–86)	20
2 **Jerry Lynch** (1954–66)	18
3 **John Vander Wal*** (1991–)	17
4=**Gates Brown** (1963–75)	16
=**Smoky Burgess** (1949–67)	16
=**Willie McCovey** (1959–80)	16
7 **George Crowe** (1952–61)	14
8=**Dave Hansen*** (1990–)	13
=**Glenallen Hill** (1989–00)	13
10=**Joe Adcock** (1950–66)	12
=**Bob Cerv** (1951–62)	12
=**Jose Morales** (1973–84)	12
=**Graig Nettles** (1967–88)	12

LAYING ONE DOWN

Brett Butler was one of the most successful bunters in recent years, combining great speed with solid technique at this often-overlooked batting skill.

THE TOP 10

Most Complete Game 1–0 Wins

PITCHER	CG 1–0 WINS
1 **Walter Johnson**	38
2 **Grover Cleveland Alexander**	17
3 **Bert Blyleven**	15
4 **Christy Mathewson**	14
5=**Eddie Plank**	13
=**Ed Walsh**	13
=**Doc White**	13
=**Cy Young**	13
=**Dean Chance**	13
10=**Stan Coveleski**	12
=**Gaylord Perry**	12
=**Steve Carlton**	12

THE TOP 10

Recent Annual Leaders in Sacrifice Bunts

YEAR	PLAYER	SAC BUNTS
2001	=**Tom Glavine***	17
	=**Ricky Gutierrez***	17
	=**Jack Wilson***	17
2000	=**Alex Gonzalez***	16
	=**Ricky Gutierrez***	16
1999	=**Shane Reynolds***	17
	=**Omar Vizquel***	17
1998	**Neifi Perez***	22
1997	**Edgar Renteria***	19
1996	**Tom Goodwin***	21
1995	**Bobby Jones**	18
1994	**Ken Hill**	16
1993	**Jose Offerman***	25
1992	**Brett Butler**	24

A sacrifice bunt is when a player makes out on a bunt in order to advance a baserunner.

THE TOP 10

Most Times Grounding into a Double Play, Single-Season

PLAYER (YEAR)	GIDP
1 **Jim Rice** (1984)	36
2 **Jim Rice** (1985)	35
3=**Ben Grieve*** (2000)	32
=**Jackie Jensen** (1954)	32
=**Cal Ripken**, Jr. (1985)	32
6=**Tony Armas** (1983)	31
=**Jim Rice** (1983)	31
=**Ivan Rodriguez*** (1999)	31
=**Bobby Doerr** (1949)	31
10=**Billy Hitchcock** (1950)	30
=**Ernie Lombardi** (1938)	30
=**Dave Winfield** (1983)	30
=**Carl Yastrzemski** (1964)	30

It's not a stat that players brag about, but it's part of the game. However, notice that most of these players are big RBI men for their teams, in some cases league leaders at some point in their careers. Their leadership in this category is an offshoot of their often being at bat with men on base. It is also a result of their hitting the ball hard, and, in most cases, their less than stellar speed.

Ten Most Career Sacrifice Flies

(Player/SFs)

❶ **Harold Baines***, 99 ❷ **Gary Carter**, 99 ❸ = **Bobby Bonilla***, 97; = **Bill Buckner**, 97 ❺ = **Ernie Banks**, 96; = **Willie Davis**, 96; = **Wade Boggs**, 96; = **Don Mattingl**y, 96; = **Joe Morgan**, 96; = **Al Oliver**, 96

A sacrifice fly is awarded to a batter when a runner advances and scores after a fly ball hit by the batter is caught. The batter receives an RBI in this case, but does not get an official at-bat.

* Active through 2001

QUIZ TIME

Many fathers and sons have played in the Major Leagues. Can you name the father-son pair of pitchers who has combined to win the most games? Answer on page 39.

ODDS & ENDS

LAST MAN
Edward "Dutch" Zwilling played two Major League and two Federal League seasons.

First 10 Players Alphabetically

PLAYER (SEASONS PLAYED)

1 **Hank Aaron** (1954–76)
2 **Tommie Aaron** (1962–71)
3 **Don Aase** (1977–90)
4 **Andy Abad*** (2001–)
5 **John Abadie** (1875)
6 **Ed Abbaticchio** (1897–1910)
7 **Bert Abbey** (1892–96)
8 **Charlie Abbey** (1893–97)
9 **Fred Abbott** (1903–05)
10 **Jim Abbott** (1989–99)

Last 10 Players Alphabetically

PLAYER (SEASONS PLAYED)

1 **Dutch Zwilling** (1910, 1914–16)
2 **George Zuverink** (1951–59)
3 **Paul Zuvella** (1982–91)
4 **Frank Zupo** (1957–61)
5 **Bob Zupcic** (1991–94)
6 **Julio Zuleta** (2000)
7 **Bill Zuber** (1936–47)
8 **Jon Zuber** (1996–98)
9 **Eddie Zosky** (1991–92, '95, '99–2000)
10 **Sam Zoldak** (1944–52)

Most Hits, Last Name Johnson
Player (Seasons Played)/Hits

1 **Bob Johnson** (1933–45), 2,051 2 **Lance Johnson** (1987–00), 1,565
3 **Deron Johnson** (1960–76), 1,447 4 **Alex Johnson** (1964–76), 1,331
5 **Cliff Johnson** (1972–86), 1,016 6 **Roy Johnson** (1929–38), 1,292
7 **Davey Johnson** (1965–78), 1,252 8 **Howard Johnson** (1982–95), 1,229
9 **Billy Johnson** (1943–53), 882 10 **Lamar Johnson** (1974–82), 755

Most Home Runs by Brothers

	PLAYERS (HRs)	TOTAL HRs
1	**Hank** (755) and **Tommie** (13) **Aaron**	768
2	**Joe** (361), **Vince** (125), and **Dom** (87) **DiMaggio**	573
3	**Jose** (462) and **Ozzie** (0) **Canseco**	462
4	**Cal** (431) and **Billy** (20) **Ripken**	451
5=	**Ken** (282) and **Clete** (162) **Boyer**	444
=	**Lee** (354) and **Carlos** (90) **May**	444
7	**Graig** (390) and **Jim** (16) **Nettles**	406
8	**Richie** (351), **Hank** (6), and **Ron** (1) **Allen**	358
8	**Bob** (288) and **Roy** (58) **Johnson**	346
10	**George** (317) and **Ken** (10) **Brett**	327

Most Pitching Wins by Brothers

	PITCHERS (WINS)	TOTAL WINS
1	**Phil** (318) and **Joe** (221) **Niekro**	539
2	**Gaylord** (314) and **Jim** (215) **Perry**	529
3	**John** (326), **Dad** (39), and **Walter** (18) **Clarkson**	383
4	**Christy** (373) and **Henry** (0) **Mathewson**	373
5	**Pud** (361) and **Lou** (0) **Galvin**	361
6	**Stan** (215) and **Harry** (81) **Coveleski**	296
7	**Bob** (168) and **Ken** (114) **Forsch**	278
8	**Ramon** (135) and **Pedro** (132) **Martinez**	267
9	**Jesse** (153) and **Virgil** (61) **Barnes**	214
10	**Rick** (211) and **Paul** (16) **Reuschel**	210

DOUBLE QUIZ TIME
What "iron" superstar holds the record for most grand slam home runs in a career? What switch-hitter slugged the most home runs? See both on 40–41.

THE TOP 10

Most Home Runs by Fathers and Sons

PLAYERS (HRS)	TOTAL HRs
1 **Bobby** (332) and **Barry*** (567) **Bonds**	899
2 **Ken, Sr.** (152) and **Ken Jr.*** (460) **Griffey**	612
3 **Tony** (379) and **Eduardo** (37) **Perez**	416
4 **Felipe** (206) and **Moises*** (202) **Alou**	408
5 **Gus** (206) and **Buddy** (201) **Bell**	407
6 **Yogi** (358) and **Dale** (9) **Berra**	367
7 **Bob** (105) and **Bret*** (151) and **Aaron*** **Boone** (42)	309
8 **Sandy Sr.** (13) **Sandy, Jr.*** (190), **Roberto*** **Alomar** (97)	309
9 **Hal** (191) and **Brian** (103) **McRae**	294
10 **Earl** (238) and **Earl, Jr.** (44) **Averill**	116

THE TOP 10

Most Pitching Wins by Fathers and Sons

FATHER/SON (CAREER WINS)	TOTAL WINS
1 **Mel, Sr.** (164) and **Todd*** (138) **Stottlemyre**	302
2 = **Dizzy** (170) and **Steve** (88) **Trout**	258
3 = **Jim** (127) and **Jim, Jr.** (97) **Bagby**	224
4 **Ed** (195) and **Ed, Jr.** (11) **Walsh**	206
5 **Joe** (52) and **Joe, Jr.** (142) **Coleman**	194
6 = **Clyde** (100) and **Jaret*** (33) **Wright**	133
7 = **Ross** (0) and **Ross, Jr.** (124) **Grimsley**	124
8 = **Julio** (7) and **Jaime** (116) **Navarro**	123
9 = **Joe** (117) and **Joe, Jr.** (0) **Wood**	117
10 **Dick** (115) and **Steve** (1) **Ellsworth**	116

THE TOP 10

Longest Surnames

ALL TIED WITH 13 LETTERS

1	**Gene DeMontreville** (1894–1904)
1	**Lee DeMontreville** (1903)
1	**Kirk Dressendorfer** (1991)
1	**Todd Hollandsworth** (1995–)
1	**Al Hollingsworth** (1935–46)
1	**Bonnie Hollingsworth** (1922–28)
1	**Austin Knickerbocker** (1947)
1	**Bill Knickerbocker** (1933–42)
1	**Lou Schiappacasse** (1902)
1	**Ossee Schreckengost** (1897–1908)
1	**William Van Landingham** (1994–97)

With a seven-letter first name, Van Landingham (right), who pitched in this very crowded jersey for the Giants, earns the top spot for longest full name of all time in baseball.

LONG NAME, SHORT CAREER

Van Landingham was a starting pitcher who finished his four-year Major League career (1994–97) with a 27–26 record.

HOME RUNS

Most Home Runs by a Righthanded Batter

BATTER (SEASONS PLAYED)	HOME RUNS
1 Hank Aaron (1954–76)	755
2 Willie Mays (1951–73)	660
3 Frank Robinson (1956–76)	586
4 Mark McGwire* (1986–)	583
5 Harmon Killebrew (1954–75)	573
6 Mike Schmidt (1972–89)	548
7 Jimmie Foxx (1925–45)	534
8 Ernie Banks (1953–71)	512
9 Dave Winfield (1973–95)	465
10 Jose Canseco* (1985–)	462

Most Home Runs by a Lefthanded Batter

BATTER (SEASONS PLAYED)	HOME RUNS
1 Babe Ruth (1914–35)	714
2 Barry Bonds* (1986–)	567
3 Reggie Jackson (1967–87)	563
4 =Willie McCovey (1959–80)	521
=Ted Williams (1939–60)	521
6 Eddie Mathews (1952–68)	512
7 Mel Ott (1926–47)	511
8 Lou Gehrig (1923–39)	493
9 =Stan Musial (1941–63)	475
=Willie Stargell (1962–82)	475

Most Consecutive Seasons with 20 or More Home Runs

PLAYER (CONSEC. SEASONS)	NO. OF SEASONS
1 Hank Aaron (1955–74)	20
2 Babe Ruth (1919–1934)	16
3 Willie Mays (1954–68)	15
4 =Eddie Mathews (1952–65)	14
=Mike Schmidt (1974–87)	14
5 =Billy Williams (1961–73)	13
=Willie Stargell (1964–76)	13
=Reggie Jackson (1968–80)	13
8 =Lou Gehrig (1927–38)	12
=Jimmie Foxx (1929–40)	12
=Frank Robinson (1956–67)	12
=Joe Carter (1986–97)	12
=Barry Bonds (1990–2001)	12

Most Home Runs by Switch Hitter

Batter (Seasons Played) Home Runs

1. Mickey Mantle (1951–68) 536
2. Eddie Murray (1977–97) 504
3. Chili Davis (1981–99) 350
4. Reggie Smith (1966–82) 314
5. Bobby Bonilla* (1986–) 287
6. Ruben Sierra* (1986–) 263
7. Ted Simmons (1968–88) 248
8. Ken Singleton (1970–84) 246
9. Mickey Tettleton (1984–97) 245
10. Ken Caminiti (1987–2001) 239

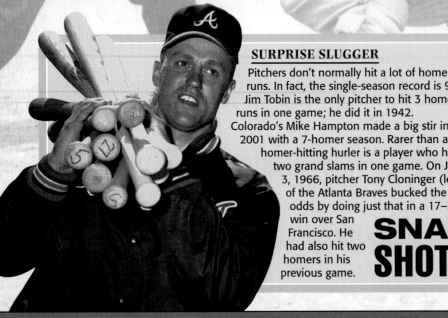

SURPRISE SLUGGER

Pitchers don't normally hit a lot of home runs. In fact, the single-season record is 9. Jim Tobin is the only pitcher to hit 3 home runs in one game; he did it in 1942. Colorado's Mike Hampton made a big stir in 2001 with a 7-homer season. Rarer than a homer-hitting hurler is a player who hits two grand slams in one game. On July 3, 1966, pitcher Tony Cloninger (left) of the Atlanta Braves bucked the odds by doing just that in a 17–3 win over San Francisco. He had also hit two homers in his previous game.

SNAP SHOTS

Most Seasons of 40 or More Home Runs

PLAYER	NO. OF SEASONS
1 Babe Ruth	11
2 =Hank Aaron	8
=Harmon Killebrew	8
4 =Ken Griffey, Jr.*	6
=Willie Mays	6
=Mark McGwire*	6
7 =Eight players tied with	5

Of the eight players tied with five, three players made the list in 2001. Barry Bonds made the list by July on the way to his record 73 home runs. Juan Gonzalez found his new home with the Indians to his liking by slugging 46 homers. And Sammy Sosa continued his amazing home run success.

* Active through 2001

Top 10 Most Recent Players Hitting Four Home Runs in a Game

	PLAYER, TEAM	DATE
1	**Mark Whiten**, St. Louis	September 7, 1993
2	**Bob Horner**, Atlanta	July 6, 1986
3	**Mike Schmidt**, Philadelphia	April 17, 1976
4	**Willie Mays**, San Francisco	April 30, 1961
5	**Rocky Colavito**, Cleveland	June 10, 1959
6	**Joe Adcock**, Milwaukee	July 31, 1954
7	**Gil Hodges**, Brooklyn	August 31, 1950
8	**Pat Seerey**, Chicago	July 18, 1948
9	**Chuck Klein**, Philadelphia	July 10, 1936
10	**Lou Gehrig**, New York	June 3, 1932

THE TOP 10

Most Career Grand Slams

	PLAYER	GRAND SLAMS
1	**Lou Gehrig**	23
2	**Willie McCovey**	18
3=	**Jimmie Foxx**	17
=	**Ted Williams**	17
=	**Robin Ventura***	17
6=	**Hank Aaron**	16
=	**Babe Ruth**	16
8=	**Gil Hodges**	14
=	**Ken Griffey, Jr.***	14
=	**Mark McGwire***	14
10=	**Joe DiMaggio**	13
=	**Ralph Kiner**	13

IN THE CLUTCH

Among his 493 career homers, Lou Gehrig had a record 23 "grand salamis." Playing on a high-scoring team like the powerful Yankees of the 1920s and 1930s helped a little.

WORD PLAY
Among the dozens of nicknames or phrases for home runs: dinger, tater, goin' yard, gonzo, four-bagger, circuit clout, big fly, round-tripper, parkin' it, long ball, jack, belt.

41

ODDS & ENDS

Best Team Nicknames

	NICKNAME (ERA, IF APPLICABLE)	TEAM
1	**Big Red Machine** (1970s)	Cincinnati Reds
2	**Bronx Bombers**	New York Yankees
3	**Old Towne Team**	Boston Red Sox
4	**The Friars**	San Diego Padres
5	**The Cardiac Kids** (1950s)	Philadelphia Phillies
6	**The Gashouse Gang** (1930s)	St. Louis Cardinals
7	**The Halos**	Anaheim Angels
8	**The Tribe**	Cleveland Indians
9	**Pale Hose**	Chicago White Sox
10	**The Lords of Flatbush** (1950s)	Brooklyn Dodgers

This is a completely subjective list, and we hope that you can think of lots of other team nicknames that deserve a mention. The list combines nicknames that were used for teams during specific eras, as well as nicknames in everyday use. Many of the nicknames were first coined by writers looking for another way to refer to the teams they covered.

A REAL VETERAN PITCHER
Satchel Paige came out of retirement in 1965 to throw one game for the Kansas City Athletics at the "tender" age of 59.

Best Nicknames, Retired Players

	PLAYER	NICKNAME
1	**Jack Chapman**	Death to Flying Things
2	**Babe Ruth***	Sultan of Swat
3	**Reggie Jackson**	Mr. October
4	**Ted Williams**	The Splendid Splinter
5	**Joe DiMaggio**	The Yankee Clipper
6	**Willie Mays**	Say Hey Kid
7	**Dick Stuart**	Dr. Strangeglove
8	**Bill Lee**	Spaceman
9	**Stan Musial**	The Man
10	**Harold Reese**	Pee Wee

This is a completely subjective list. Please feel free to make your own. There have been hundreds of great nicknames in baseball history. We chose these as the most unique and memorable. Why was Chapman called that? He was a great fielder, and made a lot of great catches. The "flying things" were baseballs! (*Babe was a nickname for George Herman Ruth.)

The Ten Most Most-Retired Numbers

(Uniform Number/Teams)

1 42, 30 **2** 4, 8 **3** = 1,7; = 20,7
5 3, 6; = 5, 6 **7** = 8, 5; = 9, 5;
= 14, 5; = 34, 5 **10** = 6, 4; = 19, 4;
= 32, 4; = 44, 4

To honor their greatest players, teams "retire" uniform numbers, meaning that no player on that team will ever wear that number again. The numbers are displayed at the ballpark, often as large signs on the outfield wall or on the bleachers. The first number retired was Lou Gehrig's number 4 in 1939 by the Yankees. In 1997, to honor Jackie Robinson on the fiftieth anniversary of his rookie season, Robinson's number 42 was officially retired by Major League Baseball.

Oldest Player, Each Position

	POSITION	PLAYER (SEASON)	AGE
1	Manager	**Connie Mack**	87
2	Pitcher	**Satchel Paige** (1965)	59
3	DH	**Minnie Miñoso** (1976)	53
4	Outfielder	**Nick Altrock** (1929)	53
5	Catcher	**Jim O'Rourke** (1904)	52
6 =	3rd Base	**Jimmy Austin** (1929)	49
=	2nd Base	**Arlie Latham** (1909)	49
8 =	1st Base	**Dan Brouthers** (1904)	46
=	1st Base	**Cap Anson** (1897)	46
10	Shortstop	**Bobby Wallace** (1918)	44

Manager is not a position, true, but otherwise our list would have been less than a "top ten."

DID YOU KNOW?
The highest retired uniform number is Carlton Fisk's number 72 by the White Sox. Fisk created that number by reversing the numerals of his old number with the Red Sox.

TEAMS

O CANADA!

Joe Carter and the Toronto Blue Jays celebrate the 1992 World Series championship, the first ever won by a team from outside the United States. They would repeat the feat the next season.

THE TOP 10

Expansion Teams with the Best First–Season Records

TEAM (YEAR)	WIN PCT. (RECORD)
1 **Angels** (1961)	.438 (70–90)
2 **Royals** (1969)	.426 (69–93)
3 **Rockies** (1993)	.414 (67–95)
4 **Diamondbacks** (1998)	.401 (65–97)
5 **Colt .45s** (1962)	.400 (64–96)
6= **Pilots** (1969)	.395 (64–98)
= **Mariners** (1977)	.395 (64–98)
= **Marlins** (1993)	.395 (64–98)
9 **Devil Rays** (1998)	.389 (63–99)
10 **Blue Jays** (1977)	.335 (54–107)

Expansion teams are formed by an expansion draft of players from other teams, as well as minor league players and college and high school draft picks. It usually takes a team several seasons to improve, but the Arizona Diamondbacks won the World Series in their fourth season.

THE TOP 10

Most Victories by a Team, All–Time

TEAM	VICTORIES
1 **N.Y./S.F. Giants**	9,676
2 **Chicago Cubs**	9,512
3 **Bos./Mil./Atl. Braves**	9,145
4 **B'klyn/L.A. Dodgers**	9,365
5 **St. Louis Cardinals**	9,296
6 **Cincinnati Reds**	9,224
7 **Pittsburgh Pirates**	9,203
8 **New York Yankees**	8,792
9 **Philadelphia Phillies**	8,339
10 **Cleveland Indians**	7,987

The Ten Newest MLB Teams
Team/Year Founded

1 = **Arizona Diamondbacks**, 1998; = **Tampa Bay Devil Rays**, 1998
3 = **Colorado Rockies**, 1993; = **Florida Marlins**, 1993 **5** = **Seattle Mariners**, 1977; = **Toronto Blue Jays**, 1977; **7** = **San Diego Padres**, 1969; = **Montreal Expos**, 1969; = **Milwaukee Brewer**s, 1969 **10** **Kansas City Royals**, 1968

Major League Baseball welcomes new teams through the "expansion" process. Ownership groups must meet hundreds of criteria before a new franchise is created. Note: The Brewers played one season as the Seattle Pilots before moving to Milwaukee.

WINNING HIT

Florida shortstop Edgar Renteria hits the game-winning single in the bottom of the 11th inning in Game 7 of the 1997 World Series, making the young Marlins the champs.

DID YOU KNOW?

The Montreal Expos were named for Expo 67, a World's Fair-like event held in Montreal two years before the team was founded.

Oldest Teams in the American League

TEAM	YEAR FOUNDED
1 =Boston Red Sox	1901
=Chicago White Sox	1901
=Cleveland Indians	1901
=Detroit Tigers	1901
=Oakland Athletics	1901
=Baltimore Orioles	1901
=Minnesota Twins	1901
=New York Yankees	1901
9 Texas Rangers	1961
10 Anaheim Angels	1961

The American League was formed in 1901 as the second Major League. Four franchises survive in their hometowns: Boston, Chicago, Cleveland, and Detroit. Only the Tigers have played their entire history with one nickname. Among other original A.L. teams, the Orioles played one season (1901) in Milwaukee before moving to St. Louis as the Browns; the Twins began play as the Washington Senators, then moved to Minnesota in 1961. The Athletics first played in Philadelphia, later moving to Kansas City and then to Oakland. Since it was created after the National League, the A.L. is still sometimes referred to as the "junior circuit."

Oldest Teams in the National League

TEAM	YEAR FOUNDED
1 =Chicago Cubs	1876
=Atlanta Braves	1876
3 =Cincinnati Reds	1882
=St. Louis Cardinals	1882
=Pittsburgh Pirates	1882
6 =San Francisco Giants	1883
=Philadelphia Phillies	1883
8 Los Angeles Dodgers	1884
9 =New York Mets	1962
=Houston Astros	1962
10 =Montreal Expos	1969
=San Diego Padres	1969

The National League was formed in 1876, and was made up of some new teams and some teams from the National Association, another pro league. The dates of "founding" for the first four teams listed note their entry in the new N.L.; all these clubs had existed in some form or another prior to that date. Also, while the Cincinnati Red Stockings were the first pro team to form in 1869, that club had no relation to the Cincinnati Reds of today.

Oldest Defunct "Major" League Franchises

TEAM	YEAR DISBANDED
1 Forest City of Rockford, Ill.	1871
2 Kekionga of Fort Wayne	1871
=White Stockings of Chicago	1871
4 =Forest City of Cleveland	1872
=Olympic of Washington D.C.	1872
=Haymakers of Troy, N.Y.	1872
=Eckford of Brooklyn	1872
=Mansfield of Middletown, Ct.	1872
9 =Maryland of Baltimore	1873
=National of Washington D.C.	1873
=Resolute of Elizabeth, N.J.	1873

These are some of the clubs that lasted only a short time in the original National Association, which played from 1871–75 and predated the National League. In those days, teams were formed by athletic clubs, i.e., the Eckford Athletic Club of Brooklyn. In baseball's early days, teams sometimes disbanded in the middle of a season or "morphed" into other franchises with the exchange of little more than a handshake between the owners or organizers. Note the small cities that had pro teams in those days, compared to the major metropolises that play host to teams today.

O CANADA!

While baseball has long been played in the Great White North, Canada did not have a Major League franchise until 1969, when the Montreal Expos joined the National League, respectively. In 1992, the Toronto Blue Jays, who played their first season in the American League in 1977, became the first team outside the United States to win the World Series, which they also won in 1993. The Expos have been less successful, reaching the NLCS in 1981. Canada also is home to minor league teams in Edmonton, Calgary, Ottawa, Vancouver, and Medicine Hat, among others.

SNAP SHOTS

TEAM RECORDS

WHATTA TEAM!
Bill Dickey, Lou Gehrig, Joe DiMaggio, and Tony Lazzeri are just four of the stars that have helped the Yankees set the record for winning percentage.

Most Victories by a Team, Single Season
Team (Year)/Victories

1. **Chicago Cubs** (1906), 116
= **Seattle Mariners** (2001), 116
3. **New York Yankees** (1998), 114
4. **Cleveland Indians** (1954), 111
5. = **Pittsburgh Pirates** (1909), 110;
= **New York Yankees** (1927), 110
7. **New York Yankees** (1961), 109;
= **Baltimore Orioles** (1969), 109
9. **Baltimore Orioles** (1970), 108
10. **New York Mets** (1986), 108

Victories in the postseason are not included. With the addition of an extra round of playoffs (the Division Series), the Yankees' total of 125 victories in 1998 is the most by any team when the regular season, playoffs, and World Series are combined.

THE TOP 10

Most Losses by a Team, Single Season*

TEAM (YEAR)	LOSSES
1 New York Mets (1962)	120
2 Philadelphia Athletics (1917)	117
3 Boston Braves (1935)	115
4 Washington Senators (1904)	113
5 =Pittsburgh Pirates (1952)	112
=New York Mets (1965)	112
7 =New York Mets (1963)	111
=Philadelphia Phillies (1941)	111
=St. Louis Browns (1939)	111
=Boston Red Sox (1932)	111

Most Runs Scored by a Team, Single Season*

TEAM (YEAR)	RUNS
1 New York Yankees (1931)	1,067
2 New York Yankees (1936)	1,065
3 New York Yankees (1930)	1,062
4 Boston Red Sox (1950)	1,027
5 Cleveland Indians (1999)	1,009
6 St. Louis Cardinals (1930)	1,004
7 New York Yankees (1932)	1,002
8 Chicago Cubs (1930)	998
9 Seattle Mariners (1996)	993
10 Chicago Cubs (1929)	982

THE TOP 10

Most Strikeouts by a Team, Single Season*

TEAM, YEAR	STRIKEOUTS
1 Chicago Cubs, 2001	1,344
2 =Arizona Diamondbacks, 2001	1,297
=New York Yankees, 2001	1,266
4 Boston Red Sox, 2001	1,259
5 Atlanta Braves, 1996	1,245
6 =Los Angeles Dodgers, 1997	1,232
=Atlanta Braves, 1998	1,232
8 Houston Astros, 2001	1,228
9 Cleveland Indians, 2001	1,218
10 New York Mets, 1990	1,217
10 San Diego Padres, 1998	1,217

QUIZ TIME?
What slugger hit the most home runs hit by a third baseman? (Answer on page 48.)

Total Games Played

TEAM (YEAR)	GAMES
1 **Chicago Cubs**	18,473
2 **Atlanta Braves**	18,443
3 **Cincinnati Reds**	18,076
4 **St. Louis Cardinals**	18,069
5 **Pittsburgh Pirates**	18,039
6 **San Francisco Giants**	17,939
7 **Philadelphia Phillies**	17,911
8 **Los Angeles Dodgers**	17,876
9 **Detroit Tigers**	15,624
10 **Minnesota Twins**	15,589

Not surprisingly, these are the oldest teams in the Major Leagues…or should we say oldest franchises? While teams may move to new homes, the MLB franchise and its records remain intact. The Braves began play in Boston and moved first to Milwaukee before settling in Atlanta in 1966. The Giants and Dodgers both played in New York until 1958. Oh, yes…the Twins? Didn't they just start playing in 1961? Yes, they did, as the Twins, but the franchise dates back to 1901, when they began play as the Washington Senators.

Top Ten Best All-Time Records, by Percentage

Team/All-Time Pct.

1 **Yankees**, .565 **2** **Giants**, .539
3 **Dodgers**, .524 **4** **Cubs**, .515
5 **Cardinals**, .514 **6** = **Red Sox**, .512;
= **Indians**, .512; = **Tigers** .511
9 = **Reds** .510; = **Pirates** .510

Winning percentage is calculated by dividing the number of wins by the number of total games. For instance, a record of 6 wins and 4 losses gives a percentage of .600 (6/10). This top 10 doesn't include recent expansion teams, otherwise the Arizona Diamondbacks, born in 1998, would be listed third all-time.

Most Shutouts Pitched by a Team, Single Season

TEAM (YEAR)	SHUTOUTS
1 = **Chicago White Sox** (1906)	32
= **Chicago Cubs** (1907)	32
= **Chicago Cubs** (1909)	32
4 = **Chicago Cubs** (1906)	30
= **St. Louis Cardinals** (1968)	30
6 **Chicago Cubs** (1908)	29
7 **Los Angeles Angels** (1964)	28
= **New York Mets** (1969)	28
9 **Cleveland Indians** (1906)	27
= **Pittsburgh Pirates** (1906)	27
= **Philadelphia Athletics** (1907)	27
= **Philadelphia Athletics** (1909)	27

Good pitching helps. The White Sox won the World Series in '06, while the Cubs won in '07 and '08.

Most Home Runs by a Team, Single Season

TEAM (YEAR)	HOME RUNS
1 **Seattle Mariners** (1997)	267
2 **Baltimore Orioles** (1996)	257
3 **Houston Astros** (2000)	249
4 **Texas Rangers** (2001)	246
5 **Seattle Mariners** (1996)	245
6 = **Seattle Mariners** (1999)	244
= **Toronto Blue Jays** (2000)	244
8 **Oakland Athletics** (1996)	243
9 **New York Yankees** (1961)	240
10 **Colorado Rockies** (1996)	239
= **Colorado Rockies** (2000)	239

Proving that a bunch of home runs does not a champion make, only one of these top ten single-season home run record-holders went on to win the World Series in the same year that they made this list. The Yankees defeated the Reds in 1961, outhomering Cincinnati 7 to 3 to help them take the title in five games.

THE MEN IN CHARGE

Manager Joe Torre (right) led the Yankees to a quartet of World Series titles; his first was in 1996 and he won three from 1992–2000. Torre is the latest in a long line of great Yankees managers. Casey Stengel led the great Yankee teams of the 1940s and 1950s (he later led the Mets to a record 120 losses in 1962). "The Old Perfesser" won seven Series, including five in a row from 1949–53. Joe McCarthy also won seven championships, including four straight from 1936–39. Miller Huggins was the Yankee skipper from 1918–1929 and won three championships. While the Yankees' players have been the main reason for their success, they have been blessed with a succession of Hall of Fame managers who molded that great talent and kept the New York Yankees winning.

SNAP SHOTS

MORE TEAM RECORDS

Most Home Runs by a Team, All-Time

	TEAM	TOTAL HOME RUNS
1	N.Y. Yankees	12,345
2	S.F./N.Y. Giants	12,188
3	Chicago Cubs	11,137
4	Bos./Mil./Atl. Braves	10,940
5	Detroit Tigers	10,785
6	Boston Red Sox	10,263
7	Phil./K.C./Oak. Athletics	10,193
8	Baltimore Orioles	10,141
9	Cincinnati Reds	10,121
10	Philadelphia Phillies	10,082

Most Stolen Bases by a Team, All-Time

	TEAM	STOLEN BASES
1	Cincinnati Reds	15,813
2	St. Louis Cardinals	15,561
3	Brook./L.A. Dodgers	15,156
4	N.Y./S.F. Giants	14,838
5	Chicago Cubs	13,919
6	Pittsburgh Pirates	13,769
7	Philadelphia Phillies	12,361
8	Bos./Mil./Atl. Braves	12,344
9	Chicago White Sox	11,627
10	Phil./K.C./Oak. Athletics	10,315

Most Stolen Bases by a Team in a Season*

	TEAM	STOLEN BASES
1	New York Giants (1911)	347
2	Oakland Athletics (1976)	341
3	New York Giants (1912)	319
4	St. Louis Cardinals (1985)	314
5	Cincinnat Reds (1910)	310
6	New York Giants (1913)	296
7	New York Giants (1905)	291
8	Cincinnati Reds (1906)	289
9=	New York Giants (1906)	288
=	New York Yankees (1910)	288

Since 1900

SLIDE, MAURY, SLIDE

Shortstop Maury Wills is safe at second with his 104th stolen base of 1962, setting a single-season record (later broken by several players) and adding to the Los Angeles Dodgers' all-time stolen-base total.

THE TOP 10

Most Days in First Place

TEAM, YEAR (POSSIBLE DAYS)*	DAYS
1 **Baltimore Orioles,** 1997 (182)	182
2= **Detroit Tigers#,** 1984 (182)	181
= **Philadelphia Phillies,** 1993 (182)	181
= **Cleveland Indians,** 1998 (181)	181
5= **Cleveland Indians,** 1999 (182)	179
= **St. Louis Cardinals,** 2000 (182)	179
7= **Cincinnati Reds,** 1970 (179)	178
= **Cincinnati Reds#,** 1990 (178)	178
9= **L.A. Dodgers,** 1974 (181)	177
= **Oakland Athletics,** 1988 (182)	177
= **Texas Rangers,** 1996 (183)	177

* Number of possible days per season in parentheses

It is a rare feat indeed for a team to win "wire to wire," that is, lead its division or league every single day of a season. But domination in the regular season doesn't always pay off with a World Series title. Of these ten teams who romped through the summer, only two (#) ended up as the overall champion.

CANADIAN ROCKIE

Colorado Rockies outfielder Larry Walker grew up playing hockey in Canada but has become one of baseball's best all-around hitters.

THE TOP 10

Most RBI by a Team, All-Time

TEAM	RBI
1 **N.Y./S.F. Giants**	76,997
2 **Chicago Cubs**	76,703
3 **Bos./Mil./Atl. Braves**	75,507
4 **St. Louis Cardinals**	73,409
5 **Pittsburgh Pirates**	73,172
6 **Cincinnati Reds**	73,111
7 **Brook./L.A. Dodgers**	71,910
8 **Philadelphia Phillies**	71,891
9 **New York Yankees**	69,390
10 **Detroit Tigers**	66,374

THE TOP 10

Most All-Time Strikeouts by a Team's Pitchers

TEAM	STRIKEOUTS
1 **Brook./L.A. Dodgers**	83,167
2 **N.Y./S.F. Giants**	81,049
3 **Chicago Cubs**	80,868
4 **Philadelphia Phillies**	76,725
5 **St. Louis Cardinals**	76,708
6 **Bos./Mil./Atl. Braves**	76,305
7 **Cincinnati Reds**	75,112
8 **Pittsburgh Pirates**	73,770
9 **New York Yankees**	71,465
10 **Cleveland Indians**	71,231

THE TOP 10

Highest Team OPS, All-Time

TEAM	ALL-TIME OPS
1 **Colorado Rockies**	811
2 **Arizona Diamondbacks**	765
3 **Seattle Mariners**	742
4 **Toronto Blue Jays**	739
5 **New York Yankees**	734
6 **Tampa Bay Devil Rays**	724
7 **Boston Red Sox**	722
8= **Detroit Tigers**	721
= **Kansas City Royals**	721
= **Florida Marlins**	721

We've included the newer teams in this top 10 to give them a chance to show off a little. The more powerful overall offenses of today's game give newer clubs an advantage in these all-time, cumulative categories. Of the teams on this list, only three (New York, Boston, and Detroit) played before 1969. For an explanation of OPS, see page 13.

It's probably not the record they're most proud of, but the Chicago Cubs hold the all-time record for most errors by a team with 27,539.

TRIPLE THREAT

"Wahoo" Sam Crawford, whose hometown of Wahoo, Nebraska, gave him his nickname, is the all-time leader with 309 triples.

THE TOP 10
Most All-Time Triples, Team

TEAM	TRIPLES
1 Pittsburgh Pirates	7,885
2 Chicago Cubs	6,694
3 St. Louis Cardinals	6,509
4 Cincinnati Reds	6,341
5 Philadelphia Phillies	5,947
6 Detroit Tigers	5,448
7 Chicago White Sox	5,052
8 New York Yankees	5,043
9 Boston Red Sox	5,015
10 Cleveland Indians	4,933

Triples are becoming more and more rare in baseball, so this list doesn't figure to change too dramatically. For many years, the Pirates benefited from the huge outfield of their enormous old ballpark, Forbes Field.

THE TOP 10
Fewest Home Runs by a Team, Single-Season*

TEAM, YEAR	HOME RUNS
1= Chicago White Sox, 1908	4
= Washington Senators, 1916	4
= Washington Senators, 1917	4
4= Philadelphia Phillies, 1902	5
= Chicago White Sox, 1907	5
= St. Louis Browns, 1918	5
7= Chicago Cubs, 1902	6
= New York Giants, 1902	6
9= Chicago White Sox, 1906	7
= Chicago White Sox, 1910	7

*(*Since 1901.)* In the years before the advent of two Major Leagues (A.L. and N.L.), several teams fell below these home run totals. In fact, the 1875 White Stockings and 1877 Cubs both completed their seasons without hitting a single home run!

THE TOP 10
Highest All-Time Fielding Percentage, Team

TEAM	PCT.
1 Arizona Diamondbacks	.984
2= Colorado Rockies	.981
= Toronto Blue Jays	.981
4= Florida Marlins	.980
= Tampa Bay Devil Rays	.980
= Seattle Mariners	.980
7 = Kansas City Royals	.979
= Milwaukee Brewers	.979
9= Houston Astros	.978
= Montreal Expos	.978
= New York Mets	.978
= Texas Rangers	.978

This list is dominated by expansion teams, for the simple reason that errors are far less common today than they once were. Fielding percentage is figured by subtracting errors from fielding chances and dividing the result by fielding chances.

Total Numbers of Minor League Teams by Year
(Year/Total)

1 2000, 246 **2** 1999, 241 **3** 1998, 242 **4** 1997, 236 **5** 1996, 218 **6** 1995, 216 **7** 1994, 216 **8** 1993, 214 **9** 1992, 212 **10** 1991, 207

The number of minor league teams has risen steadily since the late 1970s. New stadiums, new team logos, and new marketing techniques have made minor-league baseball profitable for small cities and towns around the country. The heyday of the minors came in the late 1940s, when more than 400 teams crowded the summer calendar.

DID YOU KNOW?
Branch Rickey of the St. Louis Cardinals (and later the Dodgers) is credited with making minor-league "farm systems" part of every Major League team.

WE WON! WE WON!
The New York Mets celebrate their victory in a 1999 playoff game that gave them the wild-card spot in the N.L. Division Series.

Teams with Most Hall-of-Fame Players

	TEAM	PLAYERS
1	N.Y./S.F. Giants	51
2	Bos./Mil./Atl. Braves	42
3	Bklyn./L.A. Dodgers	41
4=	Chicago Cubs	35
=	Cincinnati Reds	35
=	St. Louis Cardinals	35
7	Pittsburgh Pirates	34
8	New York Yankees	33
9	Philadelphia Phillies	31
10	Boston Red Sox	28

This list shows which teams have had the most members of the Hall of Fame play for their club at any time, including brief appearances at the end or beginning of a career. There are only 253 people associated with a team who are members of the Hall, so obviously there is a lot of overlap—many players having been on several teams during their career.

Recent Tiebreaking Playoff Games or Series

	SCORE	TIE BROKEN	DATE
1	Mets 5, Reds 0	N.L. wild card	10/4/99
2	Cubs 5, Giants 3	N.L. wild card	9/28/98
3	Mariners 9, Angels 1	A.L. West	10/2/95
4	Astros 7, Dodgers 1	N.L. West	10/6/80
5	Yankees 5, Red Sox 4	A.L. East	10/2/78
6	Giants 2, Dodgers 1#	N.L.	10/62
7	Dodgers 2, Braves 0#	N.L.	9/59
8	Giants 2, Dodgers 1#	N.L.	10/51
9	Indians 8, Red Sox 3	A.L.	10/4/48
10	Cardinals 2, Dodgers 0#	N.L.	10/46

Few things are more exciting in baseball than a final playoff game. The winning team carries on to play another day; the losing team goes home. Having two teams finish the season tied for a playoff spot is rare in baseball. When that happens, the two teams meet in a special playoff game or series. The results can be dramatic; the 1951 playoff between the Giants and Dodgers ended with Bobby Thomson's dramatic ninth-inning, three-run homer. For winners of these playoffs, the games are remembered among a team's finest moments. For the losers, they are a dark day in franchise history. (# Denotes three-game playoff series. Score is result in games.)

Most MVP Awards, Team

	TEAM	TOTAL MVP AWARDS
1	Yankees	18
2	Cardinals	13
3	Reds	11
4=	Red Sox	10
=	Dodgers	10
6	Athletics	9
7=	Tigers	8
=	Cubs	8
9=	Phillies	6
=	Pirates	6

This list records how many Most Valuable Player awards a team's players have earned since the first award was presented in 1931.

Top Ten Teams with the Most World Series Championships

	TEAM	W.S. TITLES
1	New York Yankees	26
2 =	St. Louis Cardinals	9
=	Oakland/Philadelphia Athletics	9
4	Los Angeles/Brooklyn Dodgers	6
5 =	San Francisco/New York Giants	5
=	Pittsburgh Pirates	5
=	Boston Red Sox	5
8	Detroit Tigers	4
9 =	Atlanta/Milwaukee/Boston Braves	3
=	Baltimore Orioles	3
=	Minnesota Twins/Washington Senators	3

The Yankees' total just jumps out at you...nearly three times as many as the Cardinals and Athletics. The Yankees have had mini-dynasties in the 1920s, the 1930s, the 1950s, the 1960s, and the 1990s.

BASEBALL NUT

The Phillie Phanatic does stunts on a 4-wheel ATV.

The Ten Coolest Mascots

Mascot/Team

❶ **Phillie Phanatic**, Phillies
❷ **Billy Marlin**, Marlins
❸ **Stomper the Elephant**, Athletics
❹ **The Bird**, Orioles ❺ **FredBird**, Cardinals ❻ **Pirate Parrot**, Pirates
❼ **Slugger**, Royals ❽ **Mr. Met**, Mets
❾ **Digger**, Rockies ❿ **Youppi**, Expos

This is admittedly a subjective ranking, so feel free to move them around to suit your own personal tastes. We would have included The Famous Chicken, who got his start with the San Diego Padres, but he's a freelance fowl now, not affiliated with any one team. Mascot Trivia: Billy Marlin once lost his head in a swamp. He was parachuting into the stadium before a game when his head fell off.

Most A.L. Championships

	TEAM	PENNANTS
1	New York Yankees	38
2	Athletics	15
3	Red Sox	10
4	Tigers	9
5	Orioles/Browns	7
6	Twins/Senators	6
7 =	White Sox	5
=	Indians	5
9 =	Royals	2
=	Blue Jays	2

The Athletics have won championships while based in Philadelphia and Oakland. They played in Kansas City from 1955–67, but didn't add to their total while there.

Most A.L. Championship Series Championships

	TEAM	ALCS TITLES
1	New York Yankees	9
2	Athletics	6
3	Orioles	5
4 =	Royals	2
=	Red Sox	2
=	Twins	2
=	Blue Jays	2
=	Indians	2
9 =	Brewers	1
=	Tigers	1

Since 1969, each league's champion has been the winner of the League Championship Series. Beginning in 1995, another round of playoffs, the Division Series, was added before the LCS.

MASCOT EARNS A'S
Stomper the Elephant works for peanuts.

THE TOP 10
Longest-Serving Team Owners

OWNER, TEAM, TIMESPAN	YEARS
1 = **Phillip K. Wrigley,** Cubs (1934–77)	43
= **Thomas Yawkey,** Red Sox (1933–76)	43
3 Horace Stoneham, Giants (1936–75)	39
4 = **Gene Autry,** Angels (1960–97)	37
= **August Busch, Jr.,** Cardinals (1953–89)	36
6 Clark Griffith, Senators (1969–93)	35
7 Barney Dreyfuss, Pirates (1900–32)	32
8 Charles Comiskey, White Sox (1901–31)	30
9 = **Calvin Griffith,** Senators/Twins (1956–84)	28
= **Allan H. "Bud" Selig*,** Brewers (1970–98)	28

Note: Selig left his position with the Brewers to become Commissioner of Baseball, having served as Interim Commissioner from 1993–98. If Wrigley sounds familiar, he's from the gum family and Wrigley Field is named for him.

THE TOP 10
Most N.L. Championships

TEAM	PENNANTS
1 **Brooklyn/Los Angeles Dodgers**	21
2 **New York/San Francisco Giants**	19
3 = **Boston/Milwaukee/Atlanta Braves**	17
3 **Chicago Cubs**	16
4 **St. Louis Cardinals**	15
5 = **Pittsburgh Pirates**	9
= **Cincinnati Reds**	9
8 **Philadelphia Phillies**	5
9 **New York Mets**	4
10 **San Diego Padres**	2

The Dodgers and Giants have one of baseball's oldest and fiercest rivalries. First, they battled for N.L. supremacy in New York. After moving to the West Coast simultaneously in 1958, the two clubs kept up the scrapping and maintained their rivalry. The Giants, however, have not won a Series title in the Bay Area, while the Dodgers have won five championships.

THE TOP 10
Most N.L. Championship Series Championships

TEAM	NLCS TITLES
1 = **Los Angeles Dodgers**	5
= **Cincinnati Reds**	5
= **Atlanta Braves**	5
4 **New York Mets**	4
5 = **Philadelphia Phillies**	3
= **St. Louis Cardinals**	3
7 = **Pittsburgh Pirates**	2
= **San Diego Padres**	2
9 = **San Francisco Giants**	1
= **Florida Marlins**	1
= **Arizona Diamondbacks**	1

The Braves appeared in the eight National League Championship Series in a row from 1991–99 (no NLCS held in 1994).

THE GONFALON

You are a true baseball nut if you know the meaning of that term. It is an extremely archaic version of the word "pennant," and even when people knew what it meant, it was rarely used. The pennant, of course, is the synonym for a league championship, after the huge flag given to winners. Derived from the Italian word for flag, *gonfalone*, it would have disappeared into obscurity if not for a poem. In the poem, 1908 Cubs infielders Joe Tinker, Johnny Evers, and Frank Chance are lauded for their double-play ability. The poem claims that the famous trio are "...fearlessly pricking our gonfalon bubble."

SNAP SHOTS

DID YOU KNOW?
The Arizona Diamondbacks made it to the World Series in only their fourth season, the fastest-ever trip to the Fall Classic by an expansion team.

55

TEAMS AROUND THE WORLD

THE TOP 10

International Homes of Major Leaguers

	COUNTRY OF ORIGIN	PLAYERS
1	**Dominican Republic**	79
2	**Puerto Rico**	37
3	**Venezuela**	33
4	**Mexico**	14
5	**Canada**	11
6	**Cuba**	10
7	**Panama**	9
8	**Japan**	8
9=	**Australia**	3
=	**Colombia**	3

More and more players from more and more countries are flocking to the Major Leagues. For the 2001 season, nearly 25 percent of Major Leaguers were born outside the United States, the highest percentage ever. This list reflects a ranking of the total numbers of players on 2000 Opening Day rosters from each country.

THE TOP 10

Recent Caribbean World Series Champs

	TEAM, COUNTRY	YEAR
1	**Aguilas,** Dominican Republic	2001
2	**Santurce,** Puerto Rico	2000
3	**Licey,** Dominican Republic	1999
4	**Aguilas,** Dominican Republic	1998
5	**Aguilas,** Dominican Republic	1997
6	**Culiacan**, Mexico	1996
7	**San Juan**, Puerto Rico	1995
8	**Licey**, Dominican Republic	1994
9	**Mayagüez**, Puerto Rico	1993
10	**Mayagüez**, Puerto Rico	1992

The Caribbean Series is played in the winter among league-champion clubs from Caribbean and Latin American teams. Many Major Leaguers play on these teams during their winter break.

THE TOP 10

Recent Mexican League Champions

	TEAM	YEAR
1	**Mexico City Tigres**	2001
2	**Mexico City Tigres**	2000
3	**Mexico City Diablos Rojos**	1999
4	**Oaxaca Guerreros**	1998
5	**Mexico City Tigres**	1997
6	**Monterrey Sultanes**	1996
7	**Monterrey Sultanes**	1995
8	**Mexico City Diablos Rojos**	1994
9	**Villahermosa Olmecas**	1993
10	**Mexico City Tigres**	1992

Mexico's pro league, formed in 1925, has 16 teams playing in the winter months. In recent years, stars such as slugging third baseman Vinny Castilla have joined a long list of Mexican players making an impact on the Major Leagues. Historical note: In the 1940s, the Mexican league fought an ultimately losing salary war with the Major Leagues, convincing several top stars to leave their U.S. teams and play in Mexico.

K IS FOR KOREA

The Dodgers' fireballing righthander Chan Ho Park earned the first All-Star selection for a Korean-born player in 2001.

JAPAN AIR
Yakult Swallows manager Tsutomu Wakamatsu is tossed in the air by his team after they won the 2001 Japan Series.

THE TOP 10

Most Japan Series Championships

	TEAM	CHAMPIONSHIPS
1	Yomiuri Giants	19
2	Seibu Lions	11
3	Yakult Swallows	5
4=	Hankyu Braves	3
=	Hiroshima Carp	3
6=	Nankai Hawks	2
=	Manichi/Lotte Orions	2
8	Six teams are tied with 1 championship each	

The Japanese professional league began in 1936. Today six teams play in each of the Central and Pacific Leagues; since 1950, their champions oppose each other in the postseason Japan Series. With their near-complete domination of the sport in Japan, the Yomiuri (Tokyo) Giants are the Yankees of Japanese baseball. Recently, stars such as Ichiro Suzuki, Hideo Nomo, and Kazuhiro Sasaki have moved from Japan to the U.S.

THE TOP 10

Recent Korean League Champions

	TEAM	TITLES
1	Hyundai Unicorns	2000
2	Hanwha Eagles	1999
3	Hyundai Unicorns	1998
4	Haitai Tigers	1997
5	Haitai Tigers	1996
6	OB Bears	1995
7	LG Twins	1994
8	Haitai Tigers	1993
9	Lotte Giants	1992
10	Haitai Tigers	1991

Korean pro baseball began in 1982 with the formation of the Korean Baseball Organization. The Tigers have won the most (9 of 19 through 1998) KBO titles. Dodgers pitcher Chan Ho Park is the most noted Korean player to join the Major Leagues, but several other players are training in the minors for their MLB debuts.

THE TOP 10

Recent Australian Baseball League Champions

	TEAM	SEASON
1	Western Heelers	1999–2000
2	Gold Coast Cougars	1998–99
3	Melbourne Reds	1997–98
4	Perth Heat	1996–97
5	Sydney Blues	1995–96
6	Waverly Reds	1994–95
7	Brisbane Bandits	1993–94
8	Melbourne Monarchs	1992–93
9	Gold Coast Dolphins	1991–92
10	Perth Heat	1990–91

Pro baseball is a fairly recent entrant on the busy Australian sports scene. There was an inter-state series called the Claxton Shield played from 1934–89, but a true pro league didn't start until 1989. Major Leaguers such as Dodgers pitcher Luke Prokopec, former Brewers catcher Dave Nilsson, and Expos pitcher Graeme Lloyd hail from Down Under.

THE TOP 10

Recent Japan Series Champs

	TEAM	YEAR
1	Yakult Swallows	2001
2	Yomiuri Giants	2000
3	Fukuoka Daiei Hawks	1999
4	Yokohama Bay Stars	1998
5	Yakult Swallows	1997
6	Orix Blue Wave	1996
7	Yakult Swallows	1995
8	Yomiuri Giants	1994
9	Yakult Swallows	1993
10	Seibu Lions	1992

Most Hits by a Team in One Game

	TEAM, OPPONENT	DATE	HITS
1	**Cleveland** vs. **Philadelphia** (AL) July 10, 1932 (18 inn.)		33
2	**New York** (NL) vs. **Cincinnati**	June 9, 1901	31
3 =	**New York** (NL) vs. **Philadelphia**	Sept. 2, 1925	30
=	**New York** (AL) vs. **Boston**	Sept. 28, 1923	30
5 =	**Philadelphia** (AL) vs. **Boston**	May 1, 1929	29
=	**Cleveland** vs. **St. Louis** (AL)	Aug. 12, 1948	29
=	**Chicago** (AL) vs. **Kansas City**	April 23, 1955	29
=	**Oakland** vs. **Texas**	July 1, 1979 (15 inn.)	29
9	Many times; most recent: **New York** (NL) vs. **Atlanta**	July 4, 1985 (19 inn.)	28

With the all-time record in this category coming in an extra-inning game, perhaps the Giants' 31-hit attack in only nine innings in 1901 is worth a look. That's an average of more than three hits per inning. The Giants were not exactly sluggers that season; they finished 37 games out of first that year with one of the lowest team averages in the N.L. However, the opposing Reds had the league's highest ERA and gave up the most hits. Nice timing!

Most Runs Scored by a Team in One Inning

	TEAM, OPPONENT, DATE	INNING	RUNS
1	**Chicago** (NL) vs. **Detroit**, Sept. 6, 1883	7th	18
2	**Boston** vs. **Detroit**, June 18, 1953	7th	17
3	**Boston** vs. **Baltimore**, June 18, 1894	1st	16
4 =	**Brooklyn** vs. **Cincinnati**, May 21, 1952	1st	15
=	**Hartford** vs. **New York** (NL), May 13, 1876	4th	15
6 =	**New York** (AL) vs. **Washington**, July 6, 1920	5th	14
=	**Boston** vs. **Philadelphia** (AL), July 4, 1948	7th	14
=	**Cleveland** vs. **Philadelphia** (AL), Sept. 21, 1950	1st	14
=	**Chicago** (NL) vs. **Philadephia** (NL), Aug. 25, 1922	4th	14
10	13 runs have been scored in one inning 7 times; most recent: **California** vs. **Texas**, Sept. 14, 1978	9th	13

Amazingly, the number one entry above also represents the final score. The game was a scoreless tie until Chicago busted out in the seventh. Detroit's inability to add even one run means that the game did not produce the record for most runs in an inning by both teams. That record is 19, set by the Red Sox and Indians in 1977.

Most Runs by a Team in One Game

	TEAM, OPPONENT	DATE	RUNS
1 =	**Boston** vs. **St. Louis**	June 8, 1950	29
=	**Chicago** (AL) vs. **Kansas City**	April 23, 1955	29
3	**St. Louis** vs. **Philadelphia** (NL)	July 6, 1929	28
4	**Cleveland** vs. **Boston**	July 7, 1923	27
5 =	**Cincinnati** vs. **Boston**	June 4, 1911	26
=	**Chicago** (NL) vs. **Philadelphia** (NL)	Aug. 25, 1922	26
=	**New York** (NL) vs. **Brooklyn**	April 30, 1944	26
=	**Philadelphia** vs. **New York** (NL)	April 11, 1985	26
=	**Cleveland** vs. **St. Louis**	Aug. 12, 1948	26
10	Last time: **New York** (NL) vs. **Philadelphia**	May 24, 1936	25

That the 1950 Red Sox racked up 29 runs is not too surprising. The team scored 1,027 runs on the season, fourth-most all-time and still the highest total since 1936. They led the Majors with a .302 team average and 1,665 hits. Walt Dropo set a rookie record with 144 runs batted in for the Sox that season.

BILLY BALL

Not even Hall-of-Fame slugger Billy Williams of the Cubs could stop the expansion San Diego Padres from whitewashing Chicago 19–0 in 1969.

THE TOP 10
Most Recent "Ultimate" Grand Slams

	PLAYER, TEAM	YEAR
1	**Brian Giles**, Pirates	2001
2	**Chris Hoiles**, Orioles	1996
3	**Alan Trammell**, Tigers	1998
4	**Dick Schofield**, Angels	1986
5	**Phil Bradley**, Mariners	1985
6	**Buddy Bell**, Rangers	1984
7	**Bo Diaz**, Phillies	1983
8	**Roger Freed**, Cardinals	1979
9	**Ron Lolich**, Phil.	1973
10	**Carl Taylor**, Cardinals	1970

Your team is down by three runs, it's your team's final at-bat, there are two outs, and the bases are loaded. Guess what? You're up. These are the ten most recent players to hit a game-winning grand slam in a situation just like that one.

THE TOP 10
Most Career Games with Two-Plus Home Runs

	PLAYER	GAMES
1	**Babe Ruth**	72
2	**Mark McGwire***	66
3=	**Willie Mays**	63
4=	**Henry Aaron**	62
5	**Barry Bonds***	56
5	**Jimmie Foxx**	55
7=	**Frank Robinson**	54
=	**Sammy Sosa**	54
8=	**Eddie Mathews**	49
=	**Mel Ott**	49
9=	**Harmon Killebrew**	46
=	**Mickey Mantle**	46

DOUBLE DIPPING

One home run record that the Bambino still holds is most games with two-plus homers.

THE TOP 10
Most Strikeouts in a Nine-Inning Game

	PITCHER, TEAM	DATE	STRIKEOUTS
1	**Roger Clemens***, Boston Red Sox	4/29/86	20
=	**Roger Clemens***, Boston Red Sox	9/18/96	20
=	**Kerry Wood***, Chicago Cubs	5/6/98	20
=	**Randy Johnson***, Arizona Diamondbacks	5/8/01	20
4=	**Steve Carlton**, St. Louis Cardinals	9/15/69	19
=	**Tom Seaver**, New York Mets	4/22/70	19
=	**Nolan Ryan**, California Angels	8/12/74	19
=	**David Cone***, New York Mets	10/6/91	19
=	**Randy Johnson***, Seattle Mariners	8/8/97	19
=	**Randy Johnson***, Seattle Mariners	6/24/97	19

Controversy erupted when Johnson struck out 20 in 2001. He got his 20th "K" in the ninth , but the game was not over (he didn't strike out any more batters). At first, it appeared he wouldn't get credit for tying the record, but baseball soon announced that he was officially the fourth player with 20 strikeouts in 9 innings of a game.

THE TOP 10
Most Lopsided Shutouts, since 1900

	WINNING TEAM, OPPONENT	DATE	SCORE
1	**Pittsburgh** vs. **Chicago** (NL)	Sept. 16, 1975	22-0
2=	**New York** (AL) vs. **Philadelphia** (AL)	August 13, 1939	21-0
=	**Detroit** vs. **Cleveland**	Sept. 15, 1901	21-0
4=	**Montreal** vs. **Atlanta**	July 30, 1978	19-0
=	**Los Angeles** vs. **San Diego**	June 28, 1969	19-0
=	**Chicago** (NL) vs. **San Diego**	May 13, 1969	19-0
=	**Pittsburgh** vs. **St. Louis**	Aug. 3, 1961	19-0
=	**Cleveland** vs. **Boston**	May 18, 1955	19-0
=	**Boston** vs. **Philadelphia** (AL)	April 30, 1950	19-0
=	**Chicago** (NL) vs. **New York** (NL)	June 7, 1906	19-0

Pittsburgh's smashing success over Chicago is only surprising in the total, not in the result. The Pirates won the NL East that year, while the Cubbies were 17.5 games back. Pittsburgh led the NL with 138 homers and a .402 slugging average. Chicago, meanwhile, brought up the rear in the league with a 4.50 ERA while surrendering a league-high 130 homers. Ouch.

* Active through 2001

QUIZ TIME

Everyone knows that David Cone pitched the most recent A.L. perfect game in 1999. But can you name the pitcher who threw the most recent N.L. "perfecto"? See page 64.

PERFECT GAMES

Most Recent No-Hitters by A.L. Pitchers

PITCHER, TEAM, SCORE	YEAR
1 **Hideo Nomo***, Red Sox, 3–0	2001
2 **Eric Milton***, Twins, 7–0	1999
3 **David Cone***, Yankees, 5–0#	1999
4 **David Wells***, Yankees, 4–0#	1998
5 **Kenny Rogers***, Rangers, 4–0#	1994
6 **Scott Erickson***, Twins, 6–0	1994
7 **Jim Abbott**, Yankees, 4–0	1993
8 **Chris Bosio**, Mariners, 7–0	1993
9 **Bret Saberhagen***, Royals, 7–0	1991
10 **Wilson Alvarez***, White Sox, 7–0	1991

In 2001, Hideo Nomo became the third pitcher to win no-hitters in both leagues. (#Designates a perfect game.)

Most Recent No-Hitters by N.L. Pitchers

PITCHER, TEAM, SCORE	YEAR
1 **Bud Smith***, St. Louis, 4–0	2001
1 **A. J. Burnett***, Florida, 3–0	2001
2 **Jose Jimenez***, St. Louis, 1–0	1999
3 **Francisco Cordova***/ **Ricardo Rincon***, 3–0	1997
4 **Kevin Brown***, Dodgers, 9–0	1997
5 **Hideo Nomo***, Dodgers, 9–0	1996
6 **Dwight Gooden**, Mets, 2–0	1996
7 **Al Leiter***, Marlins, 11–0	1996
8 **Ramon Martinez**, Dodgers, 7–0	1995
10 **Kent Mercker**, Braves, 6–0	1994

A couple of oddities: Burnett walked a surprising nine batters in his no-hitter. Cordova (10 innings) and Rincon (1 inning) combined for their no-hitter.

Most Recent Perfect Games

	PITCHER, TEAM	DATE
1	**David Cone**, Yankees	7/18/99
2	**David Wells**, Yankees	5/17/98
3	**Kenny Rogers**, Rangers	7/28/94
4	**Dennis Martinez**, Expos	7/28/91
5	**Tom Browning**, Reds	9/16/88
6	**Mike Witt**, Angels	9/30/84
7	**Len Barker**, Indians	5/15/81
8	**Catfish Hunter**, Athletics	5/8/68
9	**Sandy Koufax**, Dodgers	9/9/65
10	**Jim Bunning**, Phillies	6/21/64

A perfect game is baseball's rarest pitching feat. It has been accomplished only 16 times in baseball history, including only once during a World Series, by Don Larsen in 1956. Two of the "perfectos" were pitched in 1880, when underhand pitching from 45 feet away was the rule. To achieve the feat, a pitcher must retire all 27 batters he faces in a 9-inning game, and his team must score at least once to give him the win. In 1995, Pedro Martinez pitched 9 perfect innings, but his Montreal team had not scored, and he lost the perfect game in the 10th. In 1959, Pirates pitcher Harvey Haddix pitched 12 perfect innings in a 0–0 game until it was broken up in the 13th and he went on to lose.

Most Strikeouts in a Perfect Game

(Player/Strikeouts)

❶ **Sandy Koufax**, 14 ❷ **Catfish Hunter**, 11 = **Len Barker**, 11 = **Kenny Rogers***, 11 = **David Wells***, 11 ❻ **Jim Bunning**, 10 = **Mike Witt**, 10 = **David Cone***, 10 ❾ **Cy Young**, 8 ❿ **Don Larsen**, 7 = **Tom Browning**, 7

ON TOP OF THE WORLD

David Cone is carried off the field on the shoulders of his Yankees teammates after he threw a perfect game in 1999.

* Active through 2001

THE FALL CLASSIC
Reggie Jackson's 3 home runs in one game in the 1977 World Series is one of many outstanding performances by baseball's biggest stars on the game's biggest stage.

BEST OF THE BEST

CASEY'S BOYS

The Yankees under manager Casey Stengel (center) had a lot of practice celebrating. They won seven World Series titles in 10 seasons from 1949–58. They also played in and lost the 1955 and 1957 Series, adding to the Yankees' outstanding all-time record in World Series play.

THE TOP 10

Longest Time Since Last World Series Championship

	FRANCHISE	MOST RECENT TITLE	YEARS SINCE
1	Chicago Cubs	1908	93
2	Chicago White Sox	1917	84
3	Boston Red Sox	1918	83
4	Cleveland Indians	1948	53
5	New York/San Francisco Giants	1954	47
6	Pittsburgh Pirates	1979	22
7	Philadelphia Phillies	1980	21
8	St. Louis Cardinals	1982	19
9	St. Louis Browns/Baltimore Orioles	1983	18
10	Detroit Tigers	1984	17

In 1920, Boston owner Harry Frazee sold Babe Ruth to the New York Yankees for money to finance a Broadway play Frazee wanted to produce. The Sox have not won a Series since, and many say the reason is "The Curse of the Bambino," thanks to Frazee's folly. The Sox came within one strike of winning in 1986, but managed to blow it. They also had the lead in two Game 7s, but the Curse of the Bambino foiled them yet again.

THE TOP 10

All-time Best World Series Winning Percentage

	TEAM	W	L	APPEARANCES	PCT.
1	Toronto Blue Jays	2	0	2	1.000
=	Florida Marlins	1	0	1	1.000
=	Arizona Diamondbacks	1	0	1	1.000
4	Pittsburgh Pirates	5	2	7	.714
5	New York Yankees	26	12	38	.684
6	Philadelphia/Kansas City/Oakland A's	9	5	14	.643
7	St. Louis Cardinals	9	6	15	.600
8=	Cincinnati Reds	5	4	9	.556
=	Boston Red Sox	5	4	9	.556
10=	Washington Senators/Minnesota Twins	3	3	6	.500
=	New York Mets	2	2	4	.500
=	Chicago White Sox	2	2	4	.500
=	Kansas City Royals	1	1	2	.500

This list ranks annual World Series appearances, not individual World Series games.

THE HARDWARE

While players receive individual World Series rings, the team is given this official Major League Baseball World Series Championship Trophy. Redesigned before the 2000 season, the sterling-silver base features red baseball stitching. The thirty vertical stainless steel poles are each topped with a pennant that represents a Major League team. In recent years, the ceremony in which the Commissioner presents the trophy to the winning team owner and manager has moved from the crowded, noisy locker room onto a platform that is erected on the field moments after the final out, so that all the fans can share in the most special moment in baseball.

SNAP SHOTS

QUIZ TIME

Mickey Mantle holds many of the key World Series batting records, but can you name the more recent player who holds the record for all-time Series average? Answer on page 69.

THE TOP 10

Teams That Have Never Won the World Series

FRANCHISE	FIRST SEASON	LAST W.S. APP.
1 Washington Senators/ Texas Rangers	1961	—-
= Anaheim Angels	1961	—-
3 Houston Astros	1962	—-
4 = Montreal Expos	1969	—-
= Seattle Pilots/Milwaukee Brewers	1969	1982
= San Diego Padres	1969	1998
7 Seattle Mariners	1977	—-
8 Colorado Rockies	1993	—-
9 Tampa Bay Rays	1998	—-

Most Recent W.S. Champs and MVPs

YEAR	TEAM (MVP)
2001	**Arizona Diamondbacks** (Curt Schilling* and Randy Johnson*)
2000	**New York Yankees** (Derek Jeter*)
1999	**New York Yankees** (Mariano Rivera*)
1998	**New York Yankees** (Scott Brosius*)
1997	**Florida Marlins** (Livan Hernandez*)
1996	**New York Yankees** (John Wetteland)
1995	**Atlanta Braves** (Tom Glavine*)
1993	**Toronto Blue Jays** (Paul Molitor)
1992	**Toronto Blue Jays** (Pat Borders)
1991	**Minnesota Twins** (Jack Morris)

Note: The 1994 World Series was not played due to a labor dispute between players and owners that ended the season on August 12 of that year.

SURPRISE MVP

In only their fifth season, the Florida Marlins, led by pitcher Livan Hernandez, stunned baseball by winning the World Series, defeating the Cleveland Indians.

THE TOP 10

First Ten W.S. Champions

TEAM	YEAR
1 Boston Pilgrims	1903
2 New York Giants	1905
3 Chicago White Sox	1906
4 Chicago Cubs	1907
5 Chicago Cubs	1908
6 Pittsburgh Pirates	1909
7 Philadelphia Athletics	1910
8 Philadelphia Athletics	1911
9 Boston Red Sox	1912
10 Philadephia Athletics	1913

The New York Giants refused to play the American League champion Boston Pilgrims after the 1904 season, saying that the newer "junior" circuit was not worthy. The Series resumed in 1905, uninterrupted until 1994.

* Active through 2001

67

WORLD SERIES BATTING

THE TOP 10

Most Home Runs, W.S. Career

	PLAYER	HOME RUNS
1	Mickey Mantle	18
2	Babe Ruth	15
3	Yogi Berra	12
4	Duke Snider	11
5=	Reggie Jackson	10
=	Lou Gehrig	10
7=	Frank Robinson	8
=	Bill Skowron	8
=	Joe DiMaggio	8
10	Goose Goslin	7
=	Hank Bauer	7
=	Gil McDougald	7

YER OUT!

Yogi Berra, who played in more World Series games than any other player, tags out a sliding Granny Hamner of the Phillies in Game 3 of the 1950 World Series.

THE TOP 10

Most W.S. Runs Batted In, Career

	PLAYER	RBI
1	Mickey Mantle	40
2	Yogi Berra	39
3	Lou Gehrig	35
4	Babe Ruth	33
5	Joe DiMaggio	30
6	Bill Skowron	29
7	Duke Snider	26
8	Reggie Jackson	24
8	Bill Dickey	24
8	Hank Bauer	24
8	Gil McDougald	24

The Yankees have played in and won more World Series than any other team, so it's no surprise that they dominate the career batting lists. In fact, of these RBI leaders, only Duke Snider of the Brooklyn Dodgers never played for the Yankees. Jackson, of course, also recorded RBI for the Oakland Athletics, whom he helped win three Series.

THE TOP 10

Most W.S. Hits, Career

	PLAYER	HITS
1	Yogi Berra	71
2	Mickey Mantle	59
3	Frankie Frisch	58
4	Joe DiMaggio	54
5=	Pee Wee Reese	46
=	Hank Bauer	46
7=	Phil Rizzuto	45
=	Gil McDougald	45
9	Lou Gehrig	43
10=	Eddie Collins	42
=	Babe Ruth	42
=	Elston Howard	42

In his career from 1949–65, Yankees catcher and outfielder Berra played in 14 World Series, winning 10. He later went on to manage the Mets and the Yankees, and was as famous for his unusual sayings as his batting prowess. His most famous phrase was, "It ain't over 'til it's over."

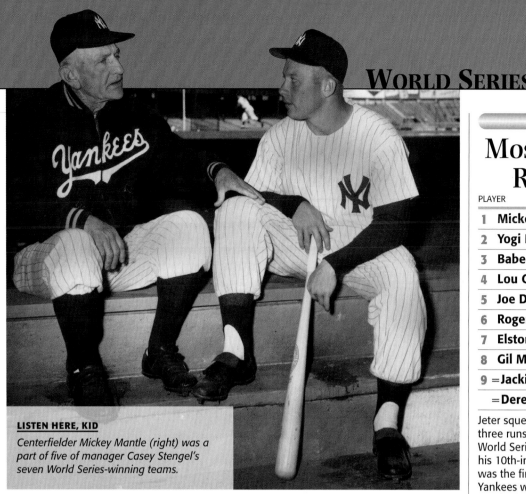

LISTEN HERE, KID
Centerfielder Mickey Mantle (right) was a part of five of manager Casey Stengel's seven World Series-winning teams.

Most W.S. Career Runs Scored

PLAYER	RUNS
1 Mickey Mantle	42
2 Yogi Berra	41
3 Babe Ruth	37
4 Lou Gehrig	30
5 Joe DiMaggio	27
6 Roger Maris	26
7 Elston Howard	25
8 Gil McDougald	23
9 =Jackie Robinson	22
=Derek Jeter	22

Jeter squeezes onto this list thanks to the three runs he scored in the dramatic 2001 World Series. One of those runs came on his 10th-inning home run to win Game 4. It was the first of two nights in a row that the Yankees would come from two runs behind to win the game.

Highest Career World Series Batting Average*

PLAYER	AVERAGE
1 =Paul Molitor	.418
=Pepper Martin	.418
3 Lou Brock	.391
4 Marquis Grissom	.390
5 =George Brett	.373
=Thurman Munson	.373
7 Hank Aaron	.364
8 Frank Baker	.363
9 Roberto Clemente	.362
10 Lou Gehrig	.361

* Minimum 50 at bats
Pepper Martin had one of baseball's coolest nicknames: "Wild Horse of the Osage."

Most Career World Series Stolen Bases

PLAYER	STEALS
1 =Lou Brock	14
=Eddie Collins	14
3 =Frank Chance	10
=Davey Lopes	10
=Phil Rizzuto	10
6 =Honus Wagner	9
=Frankie Frisch	9
8 Johnny Evers	8
9 =Roberto Alomar	7
=Joe Tinker	7
=Pepper Martin	7
=Joe Morgan	7
=Rickey Henderson	7

Most Career World Series Games Played

PLAYER	GAMES
1 Yogi Berra	75
2 Mickey Mantle	65
3 Elston Howard	54
4 =Hank Bauer	53
=Gil McDougald	53
6 Phil Rizzuto	52
7 Joe DiMaggio	51
8 Frankie Frisch	50
9 Pee Wee Reese	44
10 =Roger Maris	41
=Babe Ruth	41

Frankie Frisch, the "Fordham Flash," played in eight World Series for the Giants and Cardinals from 1919–1937.

QUIZ TIME
Mickey Mantle leads in career Series home runs. Can you name the Yankees slugger who holds the record for most home runs in a single World Series? Answer on page 70.

69

BATTING RECORDS

MR. OCTOBER

Reggie Jackson called himself "the straw that stirred the drink" of the great Yankee teams of the late 1970s. He earned another nickname, Mr. October, for his clutch hitting in the World Series. In Game 6 of the 1977 World Series, he was Mr. One for the Ages. Jackson lined the first pitch he saw in the fourth inning for a two-run homer. With two out in the fifth, he again hit the first pitch thrown to him into the seats. In the eighth, with New York leading 7–3 and only three outs away from a World Series title, Jackson smashed the first pitch for his record-tying third homer.

SNAP SHOTS

THE TOP 10
Most Hits, Single World Series

PLAYER, SERIES (NUMBER OF GAMES)	HITS
1 = Bobby Richardson, 1964 (7)	13
= Lou Brock, 1968 (7)	13
= Marty Barrett, 1986 (7)	13
4 = Billy Martin, 1953 (6)	12
= Roberto Alomar*, 1993 (6)	12
= Paul Molitor, 1993 (6)	12
= Marquis Grissom*, 1996 (6)	12
8 = Sam Rice, 1925 (7)	12
= Pepper Martin, 1931 (7)	12
= Bill Skowron, 1960 (7)	12
= Lou Brock, 1967 (7)	12
= Roberto Clemente, 1971 (7)	12
= Phil Garner, 1979 (7)	12
= Willie Stargell, 1979 (7)	12

The World Series was sometimes a best-of-eight games affair. In 1912, Buck Herzog racked up 12 hits in 8 games, while Joe Jackson had 12 hits in 8 games in 1919.

THE TOP 10
Highest Single-Series World Series Batting Average#

PLAYER, YEAR	AVERAGE
1 Billy Hatcher, 1990	.750
2 Babe Ruth, 1928	.625
3 Ricky Ledee*, 1998	.600
4 Danny Bautista*, 2001	.583
5 Chris Sabo, 1990	.563
6 = Hank Gowdy, 1914	.545
7 = Lou Gehrig, 1928	.545
8 Bret Boone*, 1999	.538
9 = Deion Sanders, 1992	.533
= Johnny Bench, 1976	.533

Minimum 10 at bats

All of these players reached these marks in 4-game World Series, except for Bautista, who had 7 hits in 12 at bats while playing in 5 games of Arizona's 7-game victory and Sanders, whose .533 was the best average in a 6-game Series.

THE TOP 10
Highest Batting Average in a 7-Game World Series#

PLAYER, YEAR	AVERAGE
1 = Phil Garner, 1979	.500
= Johnny Lindell, 1947	.500
= Pepper Martin, 1931	.500
4 Tim McCarver, 1964	.478
5 Lou Brock, 1968	.464
6 Max Carey, 1925	.458
7 Joe Harris, 1925	.440
8 Tony Perez, 1972	.435
9 Marty Barrett, 1986	.433
10 = Phil Cavarretta, 1945	.423
= Rusty Staub, 1973	.423

Minimum 21 plate appearances

This list features the players who were most successful over the course of the longest Series possible (excluding the rare 8- or 9-game Series early in the 20th century). Both Martin and Garner had 12 hits in 24 plate appearances.

THE TOP 10
Most Stolen Bases in a Single World Series

PLAYER, YEAR (NO. OF GAMES)	STOLEN BASES
1 = Lou Brock, 1967 (7)	7
= Lou Brock, 1968 (7)	7
3 = Jimmy Slagle, 1907 (5)	6
= Honus Wagner, 1909 (7)	6
= Vince Coleman, 1987 (7)	6
= Kenny Lofton*, 1995 (6)	6
7 = Frank Chance, 1908 (6)	5
= Pepper Martin, 1931 (7)	5
= Bobby Tolan, 1972 (7)	5
= Otis Nixon, 1992 (6)	5
= Deion Sanders, 1992 (6)	5

QUIZ TIME
What famous slugger is second all-time in World Series career earned run average?
Answer on page 73.

Most Runs Batted in a Single World Series

PLAYER, YEAR (NO. OF GAMES)	RBI
1 Bobby Richardson, 1960 (7)	12
2 Mickey Mantle, 1960 (7)	11
3=Sandy Alomar, Jr.*, 1997 (7)	10
=Ted Kluszewski, 1959 (6)	10
=Yogi Berra, 1956 (7)	10
6=Danny Murphy, 1910 (5)	9
=Lou Gehrig, 1928 (4)	9
=Moises Alou*, 1997 (7)	9
=Tony Fernandez*, 1993 (6)	9
=Gary Carter, 1986 (7)	9
=Dwight Evans, 1986 (7)	9
=Gene Tenace, 1972 (7)	9

Bobby Richardson was a solid second baseman for the Yankees who had surprising success during the 1960 Series, which the Yankees lost to Pittsburgh.

Most Home Runs in a Single World Series

PLAYER, YEAR (# GAMES IN SERIES)	HOME RUNS
1 Reggie Jackson, 1977 (6)	5
2=Willie Aikens, 1980 (6)	4
=Lenny Dykstra, 1993 (6)	4
=Lou Gehrig, 1928 (4)	4
=Hank Bauer, 1958 (7)	4
=Babe Ruth, 1926 (7)	4
=Duke Snider, 1952 (7)	4
=Duke Snider, 1955 (7)	4
=Gene Tenace, 1972 (7)	4
10 Many players tied with	3

Donn Clendenon of the Mets hit 3 home runs in 1969, the most in a 5-game Series.

* Active through 2001

TENACE, ANYONE?

Catcher–first baseman Gene Tenace hit only 5 home runs in the 1972 season for Oakland, so no one expected much from him in the World Series against Cincinnati. But following in a long line of unlikely Series heroes, Tenace hit 4 home runs, had 9 RBI, and batted .438, helping the A's to a seven-game triumph, their first of three consecutive World Series titles.

PITCHING RECORDS

Lowest ERA, 7-Game Series*

PITCHER, YEAR	ERA
1 **Whitey Ford**, 1960	0.00
2 **Duster Mails**, 1920	0.00
3 **Sandy Koufax**, 1965	0.38
4 **Harry Brecheen**, 1946	0.45
5 **Wild Bill Hallahan**, 1931	0.49
6 **Bret Saberhagen***, 1985	0.50
7 **Sherry Smith**, 1920	0.53
8 **Claude Osteen**, 1965	0.64
9 **Lew Burdette**, 1957	0.67
10 **Stan Coveleski**, 1920	0.67

* Minimum 14 innings pitched

A seven-game World Series is often among the most dramatic of baseball events. Starting pitchers are under enormous pressure, since they often are the linchpins of a team's success. In addition, they often have to pitch more often than they did during the regular season.

Most Career Wins

PITCHER	WINS
1 **Whitey Ford**	10
2= **Bob Gibson**	7
= **Red Ruffing**	7
= **Allie Reynolds**	7
5= **Lefty Gomez**	6
= **Chief Bender**	6
= **Waite Hoyt**	6
8= **Jack Coombs**	5
= **Mordecai Brown**	5
= **Herb Pennock**	5
= **Christy Mathewson**	5
= **Vic Raschi**	5
= **Catfish Hunter**	5

Once again, Yankee ace Ford (right) sits atop the leaderboard; he helped New York win 6 Series in the 1950s and 1960s.

Most Career Strikeouts

PITCHER	STRIKEOUTS
1 **Whitey Ford**	94
2 **Bob Gibson**	92
3 **Allie Reynolds**	62
4= **Sandy Koufax**	61
= **Red Ruffing**	61
6 **Chief Bender**	59
7 **George Earnshaw**	56
8 **John Smoltz***	52
9 **Waite Hoyt**	49
10 **Christy Mathewson**	48

Most Games Pitched

PITCHER	GAMES
1 **Whitey Ford**	22
2= **Mike Stanton***	20
3= **Mariano Rivera***	18
4 **Rollie Fingers**	16
5= **Allie Reynolds**	15
= **Bob Turley**	15
7= **Clay Carroll**	14
8= **Clem Labine**	13
= **Mark Wohlers***	13
= **Jeff Nelson***	13

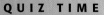

QUIZ TIME
Consider yourself a baseball expert if you know which player played in the most career regular-season games without ever appearing in a World Series. See page 75.

THE TOP 10
Lowest Career ERA#

PITCHER	ERA
1 Harry Brecheen	0.83
2 Babe Ruth	0.87
3 Sherry Smith	0.89
4 Sandy Koufax	0.95
5 Hippo Vaughn	1.00
6 Monte Pearson	1.01
7 Christy Mathewson	1.06
8 Babe Adams	1.29
9 Eddie Plank	1.32
10 Rollie Fingers	1.35

 # Minimum 25 innings pitched

Koufax, Mathewson, Vaughn, even Harry "The Cat" Brecheen—you expect to see pitchers like that on this list. But Ruth? That's right—Before he became a slugging outfielder for the Yankees, Ruth was an ace pitcher for the Red Sox, helping them win World Series titles in 1915, 1916, and 1918. He once threw a record 29 scoreless World Series innings, a record not broken until Whitey Ford did it in 1961.

THE TOP 10
Most Wins, Single World Series

PITCHER, YEAR (NO. OF GAMES)	WINS
1= Christy Mathewson, 1905 (5)	3
= Jack Coombs, 1910 (5)	3
= Babe Adams, 1909 (7)	3
= Stan Coveleski, 1920 (7)	3
= Harry Brecheen, 1946 (7)	3
= Lew Burdette, 1957 (7)	3
= Bob Gibson, 1967 (7)	3
= Mickey Lolich, 1968 (7)	3
= Randy Johnson, 2001 (7)	3
= Bill Dinneen, 1903 (8)	3
= Deacon Phillippe, 1903 (8)	3
= Smokey Joe Wood, 1912 (8)	3

In 2001, fireballing lefthander Randy Johnson earned two of his wins as expected with his performances as a starting pitcher. But in Game 7, he came out of the bullpen to shut down the Yankees. When Arizona won in the bottom of the ninth, Johnson had his third victory of the Series.

THE TOP 10
Most Career Saves

PITCHER	SAVES
1 Mariano Rivera*	8
2 Rollie Fingers	6
3= Allie Reynolds	4
= John Wetteland	4
5= Roy Face	3
= Herb Pennock	3
= Kent Tekulve	3
= Firpo Marberry	3
= Will McEnaney	3
= Todd Worrell	3
= Tug McGraw	3

A team that wins a lot of games in today's baseball needs a strong closer to shut the door on opponents in the ninth. On their way to four World Series titles in five years (1996–2000), the Yankees turned to Wetteland and Rivera. Wetteland saved all four New York victories in 1996, setting the record for most saves in a World Series. Rivera had three saves in 1998, two each in 1999 and 2000, and one in 2001.

THE TOP 10
Most Strikeouts in a Game

PITCHER, TEAM (YEAR)	STRIKEOUTS	OPPONENT
1 Bob Gibson, St. Louis (1968)	17	Detroit
2 Sandy Koufax, Los Angeles (NL) (1963)	15	New York (AL)
3 Carl Erskine, Brooklyn (1953)	14	New York (AL)
4= Bob Gibson, St. Louis (1964)	13	New York (AL) (10 inn.)
= Howard Ehmke, Philadelphia (AL) (1929)	13	Chicago (NL)
6= Walter Johnson, Washington (1924)	12	New York (NL)
= Bill Donovan Detroit (1907)	12	Chicago (NL) (12 inn.)
= Ed Walsh, Chicago (AL) (1906)	12	Chicago (NL)
= Mort Cooper, St. Louis (NL) (1944)	12	St. Louis
= Tom Seaver, New York (NL) (1973)	12	Oakland

How tough was Gibson? He told catchers who came out to chat to "get back behind the plate and just catch the ball." If that was how he treated his teammates, it's no wonder opponents feared him.

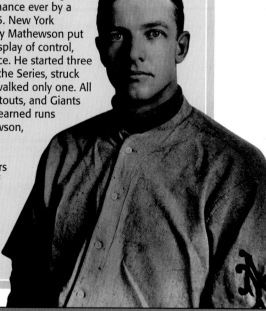

0.00

Perhaps the most remarkable single World Series performance ever by a pitcher came in 1905. New York Giants's hurler Christy Mathewson put on an unmatched display of control, power, and endurance. He started three of the five games in the Series, struck out 18 batters, and walked only one. All of his wins were shutouts, and Giants pitchers allowed no earned runs in the Series. Mathewson, renowned for his gentlemanly air, was one of the first players elected to the Hall of Fame, in 1936.

SNAP SHOTS

Active through 2001

73

Highest Attendance, Single World Series Game

	ATTENDANCE	STADIUM	YEAR, GAME
1	92,706	L.A. Coliseum	1959, Game 5
2	92,650	L.A. Coliseum	1959, Game 4
3	92,394	L.A. Coliseum	1959, Game 3
4	86,288	Cleveland Municipal	1948, Game 5
5	81,897	Cleveland Municipal	1948, Game 4
6	78,102	Cleveland Municipal	1954, Game 4
7	74,065	Yankee Stadium	1947, Game 6
8	73,977	Yankee Stadium	1956, Game 3
9	73,365	Yankee Stadium	1947, Game 1
10	71,787	Yankee Stadium	1952, Game 4

Before they moved into Dodger Stadium in 1962, the Dodgers played at the immense Los Angeles Coliseum, built to house the 1932 Olympics. Huge crowds filled the stadium to see their new hometown team deliver a World Series title.

CHAMPAGNE SHOWER
Surrounded by reporters, Pirates second baseman Bill Mazeroski celebrates the dramatic homer he hit in the bottom of the ninth inning to win Game 7 of the 1960 World Series.

Most Runs Scored by One Team, World Series Game

	TEAM, OPPONENT, DATE	RUNS
1	**New York Yankees** vs. **N.Y. Giants** 10/2/36	18
2	**New York Yankees** vs. **Pittsburgh Pirates** 10/6/60	16
3	**Toronto Blue Jays** vs. **Philadelphia Phillies** 10/20/93	15
3	**Arizona Diamondbacks** vs. **N.Y. Yankees** 11/03/2001	15
4=	**Philadelphia Phillies** vs. **Toronto Blue Jays** 10/20/93	14
=	**Florida Marlins** vs. **Cleveland Indians** 10/21/97	14
=	**Atlanta Braves** vs. **Minnesota Twins** 10/24/91	14
7=	**Nine teams tied with**	13

The most recent team to put up 13 runs was the Oakland Athletics, who outlasted the San Francisco Giants in Game 3 of the 1989 World Series. The start of this game was delayed by 10 days due to an earthquake measuring 7.1 on the Richter scale that struck the Bay Area just moments before the scheduled start of Game 3 on October 17. It was the longest gap between Series games in history and marked the first interruption for anything other than weather.

Most Lopsided World Series Wins

	TEAM, SCORE		YEAR, GAME, MARGIN	
1	**New York** (AL) 18, **New York** (NL) 4		1936, Game 2	14
2	**New York** (AL) 16, **Pittsburgh** (NL) 3		1960, Game 2	13
=	**Arizona** (NL) 15, **New York** (AL) 2		2001, Game 6	13
4=	**St. Louis** (NL) 13, **Milwaukee** (AL) 1		1982, Game 6	12
=	**Detroit** (AL) 13, **St. Louis** (NL) 1		1968, Game 6	12
=	**New York** (AL) 12, **Pittsburgh** (NL) 0		1960, Game 6	12
=	**New York** (AL) 13, **New York** (NL) 1		1951, Game 5	12
8=	**Atlanta** (NL) 12, **New York** (AL) 1		1996, Game 1	11
=	**Kansas City** (AL) 11, **St. Louis** (NL) 0		1985, Game 7	11
=	**Chicago** (AL) 11, **Los Angeles** (NL) 0		1959, Game 1	11
=	**St. Louis** (NL) 11, **Detroit** (AL) 0		1934, Game 7	11
=	**Philadelphia** (AL) 13, **New York** (NL) 2		1911, Game 6	11

The 15 runs scored by the Diamondbacks were the most ever given up by the Yankees in more than 200 World Series games.

Highest Team Batting Average in a Series

TEAM, YEAR	TEAM AVG.
1 **New York Yankees**, 1960	.338
2 **Pittsburgh Pirates**, 1979	.323
3 **Cincinnati Reds**, 1990	.317
4 **Philadelphia Athletics**, 1910	.316
5 **Cincinnati Reds**, 1976	.313
6 **New York Yankees**, 1932	.313
7 **Toronto Blue Jays**, 1993	.311
8 **New York Giants**, 1922	.309
9 **New York Yankees**, 1998	.309
10 **New York Yankees**, 1978	.306

The team with the best overall batting average in a World Series actually lost that Series! The Yankees outscored the Pirates 55–27 in seven games, but lost the Series in Game 7, 10–9, on Bill Mazeroski's famous homer in the bottom of the ninth inning.

Last 10 Players Who Hit Home Runs in their First World Series At-bat

PLAYER, TEAM	YEAR
1 **Andruw Jones***, Atlanta	1996
2 **Fred McGriff***, Atlanta	1995
3 **Ed Sprague***, Toronto	1992
4 **Eric Davis***, Cincinnati	1990
5 **Bill Bathe**, San Francisco	1989
6 **Jose Canseco***, Oakland	1988
7 **Mickey Hatcher**, Los Angeles	1988
8 **Jim Dwyer**, Baltimore	1983
9 **Bob Watson**, New York	1981
10 **Amos Otis**, Kansas City	1980

Most Games Played Without Playing in World Series

PLAYER (SEASONS PLAYED)	GAMES
1 **Andre Dawson** (1976–96)	2,627
2 **Ernie Banks** (1953–71)	2,528
3 **Billy Williams** (1959–76)	2,488
4 **Nap Lajoie** (1896–16)	2,480
5 **Rod Carew** (1967–85)	2,469
6 **Luke Appling** (1930–50)	2,422
7 **Mickey Vernon** (1939–60)	2,409
8 **Buddy Bell** (1972–89)	2,405
9 **Jack Beckley** (1970–88)	2,386
10 **Bobby Wallace** (1894–1918)	2,383

Most World Series Won by a Manager

1= **Joe McCarthy**		7
= **Casey Stengel**		7
3 **Connie Mack**		5
4= **Walter Alston**		4
= **Joe Torre**		4
6= **Sparky Anderson**		3
= **Miller Huggins**		3
= **John McGraw**		3
9= Eleven managers have led their teams to 2 titles		

George "Sparky" Anderson is the only manager to lead a team in both leagues to a Series title. He skippered the Reds in 1975 and 1976 and also ran the Tigers in 1984.

HEY, WE WON AGAIN!

Manager Joe McCarthy was blessed to lead teams with a little bit of talent…a couple of guys named Ruth and Gehrig.

LEAGUE CHAMPIONSHIP SERIES

Most Recent ALCS results

YEAR	TEAMS WITH GAMES WON
2001	Yankees 4, Mariners 1
2000	Yankees 4, Mariners 2
1999	Yankees 4, Red Sox 1
1998	Yankees 4, Indians 2
1997	Indians 4, Orioles 2
1996	Yankees 4, Orioles 1
1995	Indians 4, Mariners 2
1993	Blue Jays 4, White Sox 2
1992	Blue Jays 4, Athletics 2
1991	Twins 4, Blue Jays 1

Note: Because of work stoppage, the 1994 ALCS and NLCS were not played.

Most Recent NLCS results

YEAR	TEAMS WITH GAMES WON
2001	Diamondbacks 4, Braves 1
2000	Mets 4, Cardinals 1
1999	Braves 4, Mets 2
1998	Padres 4, Braves 2
1997	Marlins 4, Braves 2
1996	Braves 4, Cardinals 3
1995	Braves 4, Reds 0
1993	Phillies 4, Braves 2
1992	Braves 4, Pirates 3
1991	Braves 4, Pirates 3

Career LCS ERA*

	PITCHER	ERA
1	Orel Hershiser	1.52
2	Fernando Valenzuela	1.95
3	Jim Palmer	1.96
4	Don Sutton	2.02
5	Dave Stewart	2.03
6	Doug Drabek	2.05
7	Ken Holtzman	2.06
8	Tommy John	2.08
9	Curt Schilling*	2.13
10	Juan Guzman	2.27

* Minimum 30 innings pitched

Hershiser pitched in both the NLCS, for the Dodgers and Mets, and the ALCS, for the Indians. He had a 4–0 career LCS record. Palmer was 4–1 in six ALCS appearances with the Baltimore Orioles.

Most Career Strikeouts in LCS

	PITCHER	STRIKEOUTS
1	John Smoltz*	89
2=	Greg Maddux*	67
3=	Tom Glavine*	62
4	Roger Clemens*	53
5=	Orel Hershiser	47
6=	Jim Palmer	46
=	Nolan Ryan	46
8	David Cone*	45
9=	Steve Carlton	39
=	Dave Stewart	39

When your team appears in every NLCS from 1991–99, it also helps. All three of these top strikeout pitchers played for the Atlanta Braves during their remarkable run in the 1990s.

SMOKIN' SMOLTZ

Atlanta's John Smoltz has a 6–2 record with a 2.92 ERA in 17 career NLCS games. He even managed to rack up a save in 1999.

THE DIVISION SERIES

The League Championship Series was established in 1969. Beginning in 1994, Major League Baseball added another layer of playoffs to the postseason. That year, both leagues realigned to form three divisions each (East, Central, West). The champions of each division and a "wild card" team (the second-place team with the best record) move on to play in the best-of-five Divisional Series. The winners of these series then meet in their respective League Championship Series. So far, eighteen different teams have made at least one appearance in a Division Series and twelve have won at least once. Not surprisingly, the Yankees (right), with five wins, and Braves, with six, have won the most Division Series. There have only been seven seasons with Division Series, so we didn't include any top 10s. Stay tuned for further editions!

SNAP SHOTS

THE TOP 10

Most RBI in the LCS, Career

	PLAYER	RBI
1	David Justice*	27
2=	Steve Garvey	21
=	John Olerud*	21
4	Reggie Jackson	20
5=	George Brett	19
=	Graig Nettles	19
7=	Fred McGriff*	18
8=	Don Baylor	17
=	Ron Gant*	17
=	Darryl Strawberry	17

Justice has played in 46 LCS games with the Braves, Indians, and Yankees. The lefthanded-hitting slugger has an average of only .239 in those games, but he timed his hits well to amass his record RBI total.

THE TOP 10

Best Career Batting Average in the LCS*

	PLAYER	PERCENT
1	Will Clark	.468
2=	Mickey Rivers	.386
3	Pete Rose	.381
4	Dusty Baker	.371
5=	Bernie Williams*	.360
6	Steve Garvey	.356
7	Brooks Robinson	.348
8	Devon White	.347
9	George Brett	.340
10	Thurman Munson	.339

* Minimum 50 at-bats

THE TOP 10

Most Home Runs in the LCS, Career

	PLAYER	HOME RUNS
1	George Brett	9
2	Steve Garvey	8
3	Darryl Strawberry	7
=	Bernie Williams*	7
5=	Reggie Jackson	6
=	David Justice*	6
=	Manny Ramirez*	6
=	Jim Thome*	6
9=	Eight players tied with	5

Bernie Williams leaped into a third-place tie on this list with his 3-HR performance in 2001. Williams became the first player to "go yard" in three straight LCS games, including his clutch game-tying blast late in Game 4 of the ALCS.

---

* Active through 2001

QUIZ TIME

Here's a batting practice fastball that you can slam out of the park: Who was the Most Valuable Player of the 2001 All-Star Game? Answer on page 78.

77

BALLPARKS

THE TOP 10

Oldest Current MLB Ballparks

	BALLPARK	HOME TEAM	1ST YEAR
1	Fenway Park	Red Sox	1912
2	Wrigley Field	Cubs	1914
3	Yankee Stadium	Yankees	1923
4	Dodger Stadium	Dodgers	1962
5	Shea Stadium	Mets	1964
6=	Anaheim Stadium	Angels	1966
=	Busch Stadium	Cardinals	1966
8	Oakland Coliseum	Athletics	1968
9	Qualcomm Park	Padres	1969
10	Kauffman Stadium	Royals	1973

Major League Baseball has had three significant periods of ballpark construction: The 1910s, from which two ballparks survive; the 1960s, which saw several "all-purpose" fields built; and the 1990s, during which nine teams built new ballparks. Many of the newer parks combine the best of today's engineering and architectural techniques and materials with design details that recall the older parks such as Fenway and Wrigley.

THE TOP 10

Former Homes of Teams with Newest Ballparks

	BALLPARK	TEAM	YEAR OPENED	FINAL SEASON
1	Three Rivers Stadium	Pirates	1970	2000
=	County Stadium	Brewers	1970	2000
3=	Houston Astrodome	Astros	1965	1999
3=	3Com/Candlestick Park	Giants	1960	1999
=	Tiger Stadium	Tigers	1912	1999
6	Kingdome	Mariners	1977	1998
7	Atlanta-Fulton County Stadium	Braves	1966	1996
8	Mile High Stadium	Rockies	1993	1994
9=	Cleveland Stadium	Indians	1932	1993
=	Arlington Stadium	Rangers	1972	1993

Note: The Diamondbacks, Devil Rays, and Rockies were expansion teams playing their first seasons, thus did not have "former" homes. In 1994, the Indians moved into Jacobs Field and the Rangers to the Ballpark in Arlington. In 1992, the Orioles moved into Oriole Park at Camden Yards. The Houston Astrodome was the first indoor baseball stadium; the first artificial grass was called "AstroTurf."

THE TOP 10

Newest Current MLB Ballparks

	BALLPARK	HOME TEAM	1ST YEAR
1=	PNC Park	Pirates	2001
=	Miller Field	Brewers	2001
3=	Enron Field	Astros	2000
=	Pacific Bell Park	Giants	2000
=	Comerica Park	Tigers	2000
6	Safeco Field	Mariners	1999
7=	Bank One Ballpark	Diamondbacks	1998
=	Tropicana Field	Devil Rays	1998
9	Turner Field	Braves	1997
10	Coors Field	Rockies	1995

OPEN SESAME!

Toronto's Skydome (background photo), which opened in 1989, was one of the first parks built with a retractable roof. The stadium boasts a hotel in centerfield whose rooms feature a spectacular view of the field.

THE TOP 10

Largest Spring Training Sites

	BALLPARK	LOCATION	TEAM	CAPACITY
1	Tucson Electric Park	Tucson, AZ	Diamondbacks	11,000
2	Scottsdale Stadium	Scottsdale, AZ	Giants	10,500
3=	Legends Field	Tampa, FL	Yankees	10,000
=	Peoria Sports Complex	Peoria, AZ	Padres and Mariners	10,000
5	Diablo Stadium	Tempe, AZ	Angels	9,785
6	Hi Corbett Field	Tucson, AZ	Rockies	9,500
7	Disney's Wide World of Sports Complex	Kissimmee, FL	Braves	9,100
8	Maryvale Baseball Park	Phoenix, AZ	Brewers	9,000
9	HoHoKam Park	Mesa, AZ	Cubs	8,963
10	Phoenix Municipal Stadium	Phoenix, AZ	Athletics	8,500

Baseball prepares for the regular season in February and March, playing in Florida's Grapefruit League and Arizona's Cactus League.

QUIZ TIME

Can you name the Major League expansion team that set a record in 1993 for the highest single-season attendance? Answer on page 82.

THE TOP 10

Smallest Major League Ballparks

	BALLPARK	TEAM	CAPACITY
1	Fenway Park	Red Sox	33,455
2	PNC Park	Pirates	37,898
3	Wrigley Field	Cubs	38,902
4	Comerica Park	Tigers	40,120
5	Kauffman Stadium	Royals	40,259
6	Enron Field	Astros	40,950
7	Pro Player Stadium	Marlins	42,350
8	Network Associates Coliseum	Athletics	43,662
9	Tropicana Field	Devil Rays	43,819
10	Jacobs Field	Indians	43,863

When building a new ballpark, team owners want to strike a balance between a large number of seats and an atmosphere in which all fans can feel like they're a part of the game. PNC Park, for instance, is the second-smallest park, but has a real old-time feel.

THE TOP 10

Largest MLB Stadiums

	BALLPARK	LOCATION	TEAM	CAPACITY
1	Veterans Stadium	Philadelphia, PA	Phillies	62,409
2	Yankee Stadium	New York, NY	Yankees	57,546
3	Dodger Stadium	Los Angeles, CA	Dodgers	56,000
4	Qualcomm Field	San Diego, CA	Padres	56,133
5	Shea Stadium	New York, NY	Mets	55,601
6	Cinergy Field	Cincinnati, OH	Reds	52,953
7	Skydome	Toronto, Ont.	Blue Jays	50,516
8	Coors Field	Denver, CO	Rockies	50,381
9	Busch Stadium	St. Louis, MO	Cardinals	50,297
10	Ballpark in Arlington	Arlington, TX	Rangers	50,062

If this was Baseball Top 11, Turner Field in Atlanta would squeeze onto the list with a capacity of 50,062.

BASEBALL SPRINGS ETERNAL

Spring training is a great way to get a close-up look at Major League players. Smaller stadiums and fine weather are a great combination.

FACTS ABOUT FANS

Highest Single-Season Attendance

	TEAM, YEAR	ATTENDANCE
1	**Rockies**, 1993	4,483,350
2	**Blue Jays**, 1993	4,057,098
3	**Blue Jays**, 1992	4,028,318
4	**Blue Jays**, 1991	4,001,526
5	**Rockies**, 1996	3,891,014
6	**Rockies**, 1992	3,888,453
7	**Braves**, 1993	3,884,720
8	**Rockies**, 1998	3,789.347
9	**Orioles**, 1997	3,711,132
10	**Dodgers**, 1982	3,608,881

SIGN THIS, PLEASE

Tips for autograph seekers: Get there early; be polite; have a pen and what you want signed ready; try to know the players' names; understand that players can't sign forever.

Largest Single-Game Regular-Season Crowds*

	STADIUM, TEAM	DATE	ATTENDANCE
1	**Mile High Stadium**, Colorado Rockies	1993	80,227
2	**Mile High Stadium**, Colorado Rockies	1994	73,957
3	**Cleveland Stadium**, Cleveland Indians	1986	73,303
4	**Cleveland Stadium**, Cleveland Indians	1993	73,290
5	**Mile High Stadium**, Colorado Rockies	1994	73,171
6	**Cleveland Stadium**, Cleveland Indians	1994	72,470
7	**Cleveland Stadium**, Cleveland Indians	1993	72,454
8	**Mile High Stadium**, Colorado Rockies	1993	72,431
9	**Cleveland Stadium**, Cleveland Indians	1993	72,390
10	**Mile High Stadium**, Colorado Rockies	1993	72,208

*Since 1981.

Most Seasons Over 3 Million Attendance

	TEAM	SEASONS
1	**Los Angeles Dodgers**	13
2	**Colorado Rockies**	8
3	**Atlanta Braves**	6
4	**Toronto Blue Jays**	5
5	**St. Louis Cardinals**	4
6=	**New York Mets**	2
=	**Arizona Diamondbacks**	2
8=	**Minnesota Twins**	1
=	**Houson Astros**	1
=	**San Francisco Giants**	1
=	**Philadelphia Phillies**	

82

THE TOP 10

Largest Single-Game Postseason Crowds

TEAMS (HOME TEAM SECOND), GAME IN SERIES	DATE	ATTENDANCE
1 **Houston at Philadelphia**, Game 2	1980	65,476
2 **Houston at Philadelphia**, Game 1	1980	65,277
3 **Houston at San Diego#**, Game 3	1998	65,235
4 **Atlanta at San Diego**, Game 4	1998	65,052
5 **Los Angeles at Philadelphia**, Game 4	1977	64,924
6 **Houston at San Diego#**, Game 4	1998	64,898
7 **Los Angeles at Philadelphia**, Game 4	1983	64,494
8 **Milwaukee at California**, Game 1	1982	64,406
9= **Boston at California**, Game 4	1986	64,223
= **Boston at California**, Game 5	1986	64,223
10 **Boston at California**, Game 3	1986	64,206

This list does not include World Series games. For that list, see page 74. These games are all from League Championship Series, except those marked with a #, which are from the Division Series.

THE TOP 10

Coolest Ballpark Food Items

	FOOD	BALLPARK
1	**Bratwurst**	Miller Park
2	**Boog's BBQ**	Oriole Park at Camden Yards
3	**Peanuts in the shell**	Everywhere
4	**Dodger Dog**	Dodger Stadium
5	**Sundae in a helmet**	Everywhere
7	**Rocky Mountain oysters**	Coors Field
7	**Crab Cakes**	Oriole Park at Camden Yards
8	**Gordon Biersch garlic fries**	Pacific Bell Park
9	**Lobster roll**	Tropicana Field
10	**Sushi**	Edison Field (and elsewhere)

This is a completely subjective list; your favorite or coolest item might not be on it. But in our travels throughout the land of baseball, we've come to love these items more than others.

THE TOP 10

Most Popular Ballpark Food Items

FOOD

1 **Hot Dogs**

2 **Soda**

3 **Peanuts**

4 **Ice Cream**

5 **Nachos**

6 **Bottled water**

7 **Cotton candy**

8 **Pretzels**

9 **French fries**

10 **Pizza**

"Buy me some peanuts and Cracker Jack..." And a hot dog, a drink, popcorn, and... The Aramark Corporation provides concession services at six Major League stadiums, and these are the food items sold most often at ballparks nationwide.

COMFORT FOOD
A trip to the ballpark just wouldn't be complete without a hot dog smothered in mustard, ketchup, and relish. Fans can get their food at stands throughout ballparks or from vendors roaming the seating areas. Don't forget to watch the game between snacks!

KIDS AND COLLEGES

WALK-OFF HOMER
LSU's Warren Morris whoops it up as he rounds the bases after hitting a College World Series-winning home run in 1996.

Most Recent College World Series Titles

YEAR	SCHOOL
2001	Miami (FL)
2000	Louisiana State
1999	Miami (FL)
1998	Southern California
1997	Louisiana State
1996	Louisiana State
1995	Cal State Fullerton
1994	Oklahoma
1993	Louisiana State
1992	Pepperdine

The annual NCAA College World Series brings the top eight college baseball teams to Omaha, Nebraska, for a round-robin championship.

Most College World Series Titles

	SCHOOL	NO. OF TITLES (MOST RECENT)
1	USC	12 (1998)
2=	Arizona State	5 (1981)
=	Louisiana State	5 (2000)
4=	Texas	4 (1983)
=	Miami (FL)	4 (2001)
6=	Minnesota	3 (1964)
=	Arizona	3 (1986)
=	Cal State Fullerton	3 (1995)
9=	California	2 (1957)
=	Michigan	2 (1962)
=	Stanford	2 (1988)
=	Oklahoma	2 (1994)

Recent Cape Cod League Champs

YEAR	TEAM
2001	Wareham Gatemen
2000	Brewster Whitecaps
1999	Cotuit Kettleers
1998	Chatham A's
1997	Wareham Gatemen
1996	Chatham A's
1995	Cotuit Kettleers
1994	Wareham Gatemen
1993	Orleans Cardinals
1992	Chatham A's

Recent NBC World Series Winners

YEAR	TEAM
2001	Anchorage Glacier Pilots
2000	Liberal (KS) Beejays
1999	Dallas Phillies
1998	El Dorado (KS) Broncos
1997	Mat-Su (AK) Miners
1996	El Dorado (KS) Broncos
1995	Team USA
1994	Kenai (AK) Peninsula Oilers
1993	Kenai (AK) Peninsula Oilers
1992	Midlothian (IL) White Sox

First played in 1935 and held annually since in August in Wichita, Kansas, the National Baseball Congress World Series is one of the oldest semipro tournaments in the nation.

AAU Recent Winners

YEAR	TEAM
2001	Kansas City Monarchs
2000	San Diego Stars
1999	Kansas City Monarchs
1998	West Coast Yankees
1997	Baton Rouge Redsticks
1996	Austin Slam Sox
1995 =	Hartsell NC
=	Knoxville Stars
1994	Continental Blue Streaks
1993	Forest Lake, MN
1992	Cincinnati, OH

The Amateur Athletic Union holds national championships in many sports at all age levels. The teams listed here are the champions of the 18-and-under age bracket. Note: Hartsell and Knoxville tied for the title in 1995.

DID YOU KNOW?
Founded in 1885, the Cape Cod League is the oldest of several wood-bat summer leagues that college players use to hone their skills and show off for Major League scouts.

Little League World Series First Champions

YEAR	CITY, STATE
1947	**Williamsport, PA**
1948	**Lock Haven, PA**
1949	**Hammonton, NJ**
1950	**Houston, TX**
1951	**Stamford, CT**
1952	**Norwalk, CT**
1953	**Birmingham, AL**
1954	**Schenectady, NY**
1955	**Morrisville, PA**
1956	**Roswell, NM**

Little League Baseball is the world's largest youth baseball organization, boasting leagues in more than 100 countries. There are different age divisions for boys and girls in both baseball and softball. The Little League division for 11–12 year-olds is the most well known.

LLWS States/Countries with Most Titles

	STATE/COUNTRY	TITLES
1	**Chinese Taipei**	13
2	**California**	5
	=Japan	5
4	**=New Jersey**	4
	=Connecticut	4
	=Pennsylvania	4
7	**Mexico**	3
8	**=Venezuela**	2
	=New York	2
	=South Korea	2
	=Texas	2

SOLID SINGLE

Nobuhisa Baba slices a single in the bottom of the sixth inning, scoring two runs and earning Japan the 2001 Little League World Series title, defeating the U.S. champion from Apopka, Florida.

The Ten Most Recent Little League World Series Champions

Country/State/Year

❶ Tokyo, Japan, 2001 **❷ Maracaibo, Venezuela**, 2000 **❸ Osaka, Japan**, 1999 **❹ Toms River, NJ**, 1998 **❺ Guadalupe, Mexico**, 1997 **❻ Fu-Hsing, Chinese Taipei**, 1996 **❼ Shan-Hua, Chinese Taipei**, 1995 **❽ Maracaibo, Venezuela**, 1994 **❾ Long Beach, California**, 1993 **❿ Long Beach, California**, 1992

VOICE OF THE DODGERS
Vin Scully has been telling Dodger fans about their team since the days in Brooklyn.

THE TOP 10
Hall of Fame Players Turned Broadcasters

	PLAYER	TEAM
1	Richie Ashburn	Phillies
3	Don Drysdale	Angels, Dodgers
4	Al Kaline	Tigers
5	Ralph Kiner	Mets
6	Joe Morgan	ESPN
7	Jim Palmer	Orioles, ABC
8	Phil Rizzuto	Yankees
9	Tom Seaver	Yankees, Mets
10	Duke Snider	Expos

Many former players turn to broadcasting after their careers on the field are over. This list features members of the Hall of Fame who had long careers as full-time broadcasters, as opposed to players who made an occasional appearance on the air. They're listed with the team they broadcast.

THE TOP 10
Recent Winners of Frick Award

YEAR	BROADCASTER, PRIMARY TEAM
2001	Felo Ramirez, Marlins
2000	Marty Brennaman, Reds
1999	Arch McDonald, Senators
1998	Jaime Jarrin, Dodgers
1997	Jimmy Dudley, Indians
1996	Herb Carneal, Twins
1995	Bob Wolff, Senators
1994	Bob Murphy, Mets
1993	Chuck Thompson, Orioles
1992	Milo Hamilton, Astros

The Baseball Hall of Fame honors baseball broadcasters with the Ford C. Frick Award, named for the former baseball commissioner. Since 1978, 25 men have been given the award, which was first given to a pair of legendary Yankees announcers, Mel Allen and Red Barber. While millions of people have memories of their times at the ballpark, millions more "took part" in baseball's greatest moments through the words and emotions of these men.

THE TOP 10
Careers of Famous Broadcasters

	BROADCASTER	PRIMARY TEAMS	CAREER
1	Vin Scully	Dodgers	1950–2001*
2	Red Barber	Dodgers, Yankees	1934–66
3	Mel Allen	Yankees	1939–64
4	Harry Caray	Cardinals, White Sox, Cubs	1945–97
5	Ernie Harwell	Tigers	1948–2001*
6	Curt Gowdy	Red Sox,	1949–86
7	Jack Buck	Cardinals	1954–2001*
8	Ralph Kiner	Mets	1962–2001*
9	Harry Kalas	Phillies	1965–2001*
10	Jaime Jarrin	Dodgers (Spanish)	1959–2001*

Ever since the invention of radio, baseball fans have enjoyed listening to games described by some of the best announcers around. This list is a gathering of the most well-known, listing the careers and primary teams of some of the best "men at the mike." (*Denotes working through 2001 season.)

PRE-PRESIDENTIAL ADDRESS
Before he enjoyed a career in Hollywood as an actor and a career in politics as a governor and President, Ronald Reagan put his vocal skills to work on radio as a baseball announcer. In those early days of the medium, however, announcers didn't always travel to the games. Instead, Reagan and others "re-created" the game as it was sent to them via telegraph. They would have to make their own sound effects and create their own colorful word pictures of a game that they couldn't see. If the telegraph went down, he would have to make up the game.

SNAP SHOTS

DID YOU KNOW?
The first Major League game broadcast on TV came on August 26, 1939. Only about 400 people in New York had TV sets to watch the Reds-Dodgers game.

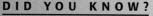

THE TOP 10

Most Recent Winners of Spink Award

YEAR	WRITER/PRIMARY NEWSPAPER
2000	**Ross Newhan**, Los Angeles Times
1999	**Hal Lebovitz**, Cleveland News and Plain Dealer
1998	**Bob Stevens**, San Francisco Chronicle
1997	**Sam Lacy**, Baltimore Afro-American
1996	**Charles Feeney**, Pittsburgh Post-Gazette
1995	**Joseph Durso**, New York Times
1993	**Wendell Smith**, Pittsburgh Courier
1992	**Leonard Koppett**, New York Post, Herald-Tribune, and Times
1992	**Bus Saidt**, Trenton Times
1991	**Ritter Collett**, Dayton Daily New

The Hall of Fame recognizes writers for long and dedicated service to baseball, combined with excellence at their craft, with the J.G. Taylor Spink Award, named for the founder of *The Sporting News*. First presented in 1962, the award has since been given to a total of 52 writers, reporters, editors, or columnists.

THE TOP 10

Our Favorite Baseball Movies

	MOVIE	FEATURING	YEAR RELEASED
1	**The Natural**	Robert Redford	1984
2	**Field of Dreams**	Kevin Costner	1989
3	**Bull Durham**	Kevin Costner	1988
4	**Eight Men Out**	John Cusack	1988
5	**Long Gone**	William Petersen	1987
6	**A League of Their Own**	Madonna	1992
7	**The Pride of the Yankees**	Gary Cooper	1942
8	**Bang the Drum Slowly**	Robert DeNiro	1973
9	**Major League**	Charlie Sheen	1989
10	**Bad News Bears**	Walter Matthau	1976

The Natural was based on a novel by Bernard Malamud; in the book, the character played by Redford, Roy Hobbs, doesn't homer at the end of the story, but rather strikes out. *Field of Dreams* also was based on a novel; the "magical" baseball field that Costner's character built is still standing in Dyersville, Iowa, and remains a popular tourist attraction. For *The Pride of the Yankees*, Cooper had to learn to bat, but he was a better actor than a hitter.

THE TOP 10

Our Favorite Baseball Books

	MOVIE	AUTHOR	YEAR PUBLISHED
1	**Total Baseball VII**	Pete Palmer, John Thorn, Michael Gershman	2001
2	**Summer of '49**	David Halberstam	1989
3	**Eight Men Out**	Eliot Asinof	1977
4	**Nine Innings**	Daniel Okrent	1984
5	**The Dickson Baseball Dictionary**	Paul Dickson	2001
6	**The Glory of Their Times**	Lawrence Ritter	1966
7	**Nine Sides of the Diamond**	David Falkner	1990
8	**Good Enough to Dream**	Roger Kahn	1985
9	**Baseball: The Golden Age**	Harold Seymour	1971
10	**Baseball: An Illus. History**	Burns/Ward	1999

A very subjective list. What are your favorites?

THE NATURAL
Robert Redford starred as slugger Roy Hobbs, who had one moment in the sun.

Most Recent N.L. Managers of the Year

MANAGER, TEAM

2001	**Larry Bowa,** Phillies
2000	**Dusty Baker,** Giants
1999	**Jack McKeon,** Reds
1998	**Larry Dierker,** Astros
1997	**Dusty Baker,** Giants
1996	**Bruce Bochy,** Padres
1995	**Don Baylor,** Rockies
1994	**Felipe Alou,** Expos
1993	**Dusty Baker,** Giants
1992	**Jim Leyland,** Pirates

This award is based on the performance of a team during the regular season and is normally given to a manager who has "turned around" a team. Voters often look for a manager who, rather than guiding a team of superstars to success, has molded a younger team to new heights or inspired a team with a poor record one year to become a winner the next.

GIANT OF A MANAGER

Former Dodgers outfielder Dusty Baker became the manager of the Giants in 1993 and has led them to the playoffs twice.

THE COMMISSIONER

This book does not contain a list of the top 10 Major League Baseball commissioners for one good reason: There have only been nine. The office of Commissioner was created in 1920 following the Black Sox scandal in the 1919 World Series. Judge Kenesaw Mountain Landis (left) was named the first to hold the office, which oversees all aspects of Major League Baseball. He held the job until 1944. Other former commissioners include Ford Frick, Bowie Kuhn, former Los Angeles Olympics chief Peter Ueberroth, former Yale president A. Bartlett Giamatti, and Fay Vincent. Currently, the Commissioner is Allan H. "Bud" Selig, the former president of the Milwaukee Brewers.

SNAP SHOTS

Most Recent A.L. Managers of the Year

MANAGER, TEAM

2001	**Lou Piniella,** Mariners
2000	**Jerry Manuel,** White Sox
1999	**Jimy Williams,** Red Sox
1998	**Joe Torre,** Yankees
1997	**Davey Johnson,** Orioles
1996	**= Johnny Oates,** Rangers
	= Joe Torre, Yankees
1995	**Lou Piniella,** Mariners
1994	**Buck Showalter,** Yankees
1993	**Gene Lamont,** White Sox
1992	**Tony LaRussa,** Athletics

Like the National League award, this award is named via a vote of the members of the Baseball Writers Association of America. There is one winner for each league.

DID YOU KNOW?
Hall of Fame catcher Yogi Berra became a manager with the Yankees and Mets. One of his most famous sayings was "It ain't over 'til it's over." Now, Yogi, this book is over.

THE TOP 10

Satchel Paige's Rules on How to Stay Young

1 Avoid fried meats which angry up the blood.

2 If your stomach disputes you, lie down and pacify it with cool thoughts.

3 Keep the juices flowing by jangling around gently as you move.

4 Go very light on the vices, such as carrying on in society. The social ramble ain't restful.

5 Avoid running at all times.

6 Don't look back. Something might be gaining on you.

Ol' Satch, the great Negro League and Major League pitcher, only came up with six in this famous "list for living," which is etched into the stone over his grave. But we won't hold that against him.

THE TOP 10

Most Recent Number-One Draft Picks

PLAYER, POSITION, TEAM

2001	**Joe Mauer**, C, Twins
2000	**Adrian Gonzalez**, 1B, Marlins
1999	**Josh Hamilton**, OF, Devil Rays
1998	**Pat Burrell**, 3B, Phillies
1997	**Matt Anderson**, P, Tigers
1996	**Kris Benson**, P, Pirates
1995	**Darin Erstad**, OF, Angels
1994	**Paul Wilson**, P, Mets
1993	**Alex Rodriguez**, SS, Mariners
1992	**Phil Nevin**, 3B, Astros

THE TOP 10

First Ten Number-One Draft Picks

PLAYER, POSITION, TEAM

1965	**Rick Monday**, OF, Athletics
1966	**Steve Chilcott**, P, Mets
1967	**Ron Blomberg**, 1B, Yankees
1968	**Tim Foli**, SS, Mets
1969	**Jeff Burroughs**, OF, Senators
1970	**Mike Ivie**, C, Padres
1971	**Danny Goodwin**, C, White Sox
1972	**Dave Roberts**, 3B, Padres
1973	**David Clyde**, P, Rangers
1974	**Bill Almon**, SS, Padres

Each June, Major League Baseball holds its annual amateur draft. Players are drafted as seniors in high school, or after they have completed three seasons in college. It is very rare for even a very high draft pick to jump directly to the big leagues. The first amateur draft was held in 1965.

THE TOP 10

Herb Pennock's Ten Commandments of Pitching

1 Develop your faculty of observation.

2 Conserve your energy.

3 Make contact with players, especially catchers and infielders, and listen to what they have to say.

4 Work everlastingly for control.

5 When you are on the field, always have a baseball in your hand and don't slouch around. Run for a ball.

6 Keep studying the hitters for their weak and strong points. Keep talking with your catchers.

7 Watch your physical condition and your mode of living.

8 Always pitch to the catcher and not the hitter. Keep your eye on that catcher and make him your target before letting the ball go.

9 Find your easiest way to pitch, your most comfortable delivery and stick to it.

10 Work for what is called a rag arm. A loose arm can pitch overhanded, side arm, three quarter, underhanded, any old way, to suit the situation at hand.

HINTS FROM HERB

Pennock was a Hall-of-Fame pitcher with the Athletics, Red Sox, and Yankees from 1912–36. He wrote this list sometime in the 1940s.

INDEX

INDEX

INDEX

PHOTO CREDITS

8–9	Mickey Mantle: AP/Wide World; Martinez: Michael Zagaris/MLB Photos
10–11	Aaron, Ruth/Gehrig: AP/Wide World
12–13	McGwire: Rich Pilling/MLB Photos; Maris: AP/Wide World
14–15	Ripken: Brad Mangin/MLB Photos;Gehrig: AP/Wide World
16–17	Clemens:David Durochik/MLB Photos; Louis Deluca/MLB Photos; Young: National Baseball Library
18–19	Smith: Don Smith/MLB Photos
20–21	Robinson: Corbis/Bettmann; Vizquel: Rich Pilling/MLB Photos
22–23	Jones: Allen Kee/MLB Photos; Rodriguez: John Williamson/MLB Photos
24–25	Mays (2): AP/Wide World
26–27	Buckner: Rich Pilling/MLB Photos; Clemente: MLB/Photofile
28–29	Wambsganns: National Baseball Library; Roberts: AP/Wide World
30–31	Piazza: Stephen Green/MLB Photos; Hornsby: National Baseball Library

32–33	1939 class: National Baseball Library; Koufax: AP/Wide World
34–35	Gibson, Ward: National Baseball Library; Paige: AP/Wide World
36–37	Butler: Rich Pilling/MLB
38–39	Zwilling: National Baseball Library; Van Landingham: Brad Mangin/MLB
40–41	Gehrig: AP/Wide World; Cloninger: Corbis/Bettmann
42–43	Paige: AP/Wide World; Jays: MLB Photos
44–45	Renteria: Rich Pilling/MLB Photos
46–47	Yankees: AP/Wide World; Torre: Stephen Green/MLB Photos
48–49	Schmidt: Rich Pilling/MLB Photos; Lofton: AP/Wide World
50–51	Walker, Wills: AP/Wide World
52–53	Game: AP/Wide World; Crawford: National Baseball Library
54–55	Mascots (2): MLB Photos; Pennant: Russ McConnell
56–57	O'Malley: AP/Wide World; Park: Brad Mangin/MLB
58	Suzuki: John Williamson/MLB Photos; Cuban players: AP/Wide World

60–61	Bonds, Mussina: AP/Wide World
62–63	Williams: MLB Photos; Ruth: AP/Wide World
64	Cone: David Seelig/MLB Photos
66–67	Yankees: AP/Wide World; Hernandez: Michael Zagaris/MLB Photos; Trophy: MLB Photos
68–69	Stengel/Mantle, Berra: AP/Wide World
70–71	Jackson, Tenace: AP/Wide World
72–73	Whitey Ford: MLB Photos; Mathewson: National Baseball Library
74–75	Mazeroski, McCarthy: AP/Wide World
76–77	Smoltz: Stephen Green/MLB; Williams: Rich Pilling/MLB
78	Williams: AP/Wide World
80–81	Skydome: Robert Skeoch/MLB Photos; Spring training: MLB Photos
82–83	Fans, kid: Rich Pilling/MLB
84–85	College World Series, Little League World Series: AP/Wide World
86–87	Scully: Bob Rosato/MLB; Reagan: AP/Wide World
88–89	Pennock: AP/Wide World; Landis: National Baseball Library; Baker: MLB Photos

SOURCES

As noted in the Introduction, most of the statistical information in this book came from Major League Baseball's official Web site, www.mlb.com. Other information was gleaned from *Total Baseball*, the official encyclopedia of Major League Baseball.

The Elias Sports Bureau in New York City is the official statistician for Major League Baseball. They provided MLB with all the stats listed on the Web site as well as all records kept and distributed by MLB during the regular season and postseason. Elias also provided us directly with some Top 10s, including those relating to game length.

The Society for American Baseball Research (SABR) was very helpful, providing assistance in locating some of the more obscure information. Special thanks to Jim Charlton for his help.

The Web sites www.baseball-almanac.com and www.latinobaseball.com and the Baseball Hall of Fame archive library on-line were also sources for some material. Web sites for the National Baseball Congress, Little League Baseball, and the Amateur Athletic Union also provided information.

The Sporting News Complete Baseball Record Book, another official Major League Baseball publication, was a font of information. We used the 2001 edition.

Other books we consulted while searching for our information included *Baseball Timeline*, by Burt Solomon, a day-by-day history of baseball; *The Series*, a complete record of the World Series, including box scores of every game, published by *The Sporting News*; *Blackball Stars* by John B. Holway, a history of Negro League Baseball; *A Whole New Ball Game: The Story of the All-American Girls Professional Baseball League*, by Sue Macy.

ACKNOWLEDGMENTS

Special thanks to Eric Enders at the National Baseball Hall of Fame for his outstanding ninth-inning fact-checking.

At DK, thanks to editor Beth Sutinis and publisher Andrew Berkhut for their continued support of our efforts. Thanks to Megan Clayton for shepherding the pages through the production process.

Thanks to Rich Pilling and Paul Cunningham of Major League Baseball Photos, Carolyn McMahon at AP/Wide World Photos, and Bill Burdick at the National Baseball Hall of Fame.

Special thanks to the the broad-backed Chris Koeper of the Santa Barbara Foresters for posing for our cover photo.

For providing all of us fans with another amazing season, full of record-breaking feats and memorable, historic games, thanks to all the players, coaches, and teams of Major League Baseball.

AUTHORS' BIOGRAPHIES

James Buckley, Jr., has written more than 25 books about sports for young people and adults, including *Eyewitness Baseball, The Visual Dictionary of Baseball, Baseball: A Celebration,* and *Perfect: The Story of Baseball's 16 Perfect Games*. He is the editorial director of the Shoreline Publishing Group, based in Santa Barbara, California.

David Fischer, a New Jersey-based author, has written several sports books, including *A Thing or Two About Baseball, Do Curve Balls Really Curve?,* and *The 50 Coolest Jobs in Sports*. He has been published in *Sports Illustrated for Kids, The New York Times,* and *Yankees Magazine,* and has worked for *Sports Illustrated,* NBC Sports, and The National Sports Daily.